Adam Smith and The Wealth of Nations

Engraving from *The Pictorial History of England: Being a History of the People as well as a History of the Kingdom*, Vol. V, by George L. Craik and Charles MacFarlane (London: Charles Knight, Publisher, 1847).

Adam Smith
and the
Wealth of Nations

1776-1976 Bicentennial Essays

edited and with an Introduction by
Fred R. Glahe

UNIVERSITY OF COLORADO

COLORADO ASSOCIATED UNIVERSITY PRESS

BOULDER, COLORADO

Copyright © 1978 by
COLORADO ASSOCIATED UNIVERSITY PRESS
Boulder, Colorado
International Standard Book Number: 0-87081-108-8
Library of Congress Card Catalog Number: 77-91609
Printed in the United States of America
Designed by Dave Comstock

To
John Van Sickle

I T is appropriate that the publication of a series of essays on Adam Smith be dedicated to John Van Sickle. Like Smith, he was both a scholar and a truly civilized human being. Like Smith as well, he was a man of the world, a universalist in his thinking. (To the envy of all of us lesser linguists, from his years as European secretary of the Rockefeller Foundation he spoke flawless French and German.) His interest was always in the species and not just one subset, geographically defined.

His boyhood years before World War I were spent in Colorado and it was there that he returned in retirement. His degrees were from two impeccable sources, Haverford and Harvard. After some years of teaching at the University of Michigan (where he met his wife-to-be, Pat) he began his European years with the Rockefeller Foundation, and later, the Social Science Research Council. In these roles he was instrumental in bringing to the United States for short or long stays many of the distinguished European scholars who were to add such lustre to the world of American scholarship from the 1930s on. He returned to teaching at Vanderbilt University in the late 1930s and then at Wabash College from 1946 until his retirement.

Throughout his career, he was a thoughtful and effective student and teacher of that freedom which Adam Smith termed one of "the most sacred rights of mankind." His publications were few—but Smith himself would never have met the publication requirements for tenure at even the most intellectually impoverished university of today. John Van Sickle knew and could put in writing the case for the free society; in some areas, such as the effect of a legislated minimum wage on regional patterns of economic activity and employment, he was, in fact, one of the vanguard. But his most important contribution was in expediting the works of others, as in his work for the Rockefeller Foundation and the Social Science Research Council; as in his planning and organizing role with the Earhart Fellows Program of the Earhart Foundation; as in his role as director of a series of summer seminars at Wabash College, sponsored by the Volker Fund (from which came, among other things, Milton Friedman's *Capitalism and Freedom*); as in his role as originator of the Principles of Freedom publication series; as in his formal and informal roles in the Mont Pelerin Society, and on and on.

He loved good wine, a good table and good conversation. He would have been a warm and enthusiastic participant in the discussions that set the stage for this publication—and embarrassed yet thoroughly delighted at the fact of its being dedicated to him. As one who taught with him, learned from him and loved him, I am greatly pleased at this opportunity to salute John Van Sickle.

Ben A. Rogge

WABASH COLLEGE
CRAWFORDSVILLE, INDIANA

Contents

Preface

THE publication of this collection of essays grew out of a series of lectures celebrating the bicentenary of the publication of *The Wealth of Nations*. These lectures were jointly held at Ohio University and the University of Colorado and were funded by grants from the Earhart Foundation. The essays in this volume by Harry G. Johnson, Joseph J. Spengler, James M. Buchanan, Leonard Billet, Ronald Max Hartwell, and Thomas Sowell derive from the lectures which they presented in this series.

Milton Friedman's essay was originally presented at the meeting of the Mont Pelerin Society held in St. Andrews, Scotland, August 22-28, 1976. It has previously been printed as a publication of the International Institute for Economic Research, Los Angeles, and is reprinted with permission. William J. Baumol's essay originally appeared in *The American Economist*, Fall 1976, and is reprinted with the permission of Omicron Delta Epsilon, the international honor society in economics. James M. Buchanan's essay has appeared in the January 1976 issue of *The Journal of Legal Studies* and is reprinted with permission. Thomas Sowell's essay will also appear in the forthcoming *Adam Smith and Modern Political Economy*, edited by Gerald P. O'Driscoll, Jr. and published by Iowa State University Press, and is reprinted with permission.

I especially wish to thank Professor Benjamin Rogge of Wabash College, who suggested the possibility of obtaining funding for the lecture series out of which this volume grew;

Mr. Richard Ware, president of the Earhart Foundation, and Antony T. Sullivan, program officer, for their support and continued encouragement. I also wish to acknowledge the assistance and cooperation of Professors Richard K. Vedder and David C. Klingaman, my counterparts in the lecture series held at Ohio University.

Introduction

IN London on March 9, 1776 the first edition of Adam Smith's *An Inquiry Into The Nature And Causes Of The Wealth Of Nations* was published. Shortly thereafter Smith received a congratulatory letter from his friend David Hume saying: *"Euge! Belle!* Dear Mr. Smith—I am much pleased with your performance, and the perusal of it has taken me from a state of great anxiety. It was a work of so much expectation, by yourself, by your friends, and by the public, that I trembled for its appearance, but am now much relieved." However, Hume then went on to caution Smith that he should not be disappointed if sales were slow at first, remarking: "Not but that the reading of it necessarily requires so much attention, and the public is disposed to give so little, that I shall still doubt for some time of its being at first very popular, but it has depth and solidity and acuteness, and is so much illustrated by curious facts that it must at last attract the public attention." Hume was to be proven wrong, for the first edition was sold out in six months and *The Wealth of Nations* went through five British editions in Smith's lifetime. It was first translated into German in 1776; Danish, 1779-80; French, 1779-80; Italian, 1780; and Spanish, 1794. The first American edition of *The Wealth of Nations* was published in Philadelphia in 1789, and it has remained in continuous publication since 1776. These facts concerning the publication record of *The Wealth of Nations* bear the most meaningful form of witness to its importance and enduring worth.

The collection of essays in this volume, which celebrates the bicentenary of *The Wealth of Nations,* are by some of the ablest contemporary economists and Smithian scholars. It is hoped that if future generations are allowed to celebrate the tricentenary in such diverse climes as St. Andrews, Scotland, and Boulder, Colorado, this collection will not only be useful for the contributors' appraisal of Smith and his vision, but will also serve as a reflection of the concerns and views of economists in the latter half of the twentieth century.

In the lead essay, "Adam Smith's Relevance for 1976," Milton Friedman persuasively argues that the economic principles set forth in *The Wealth of Nations* are just as valid today as they were in Smith's time. To document his case, Friedman cites contemporary American examples such as presidential election politics, the Humphrey-Hawkins bill, revenue sharing, and government intervention in business. However, all is not praise for *The Wealth of Nations* and Friedman is compelled to admit that Smith's advocacy of state intervention into the regulation of interest rates is inconsistent with Smith's paradigm and that Smith's advocacy of public works is in certain cases logically flawed and responsible for much current mischief. Friedman concludes his essay by pointing out that Smith's great importance for 1976 and his great achievement "was the doctrine of the 'invisible hand,' his vision of the way in which the voluntary actions of millions of individuals can be coordinated through a price system without central direction."

Harry G. Johnson, in his essay, "The Individual and the State: Some Contemporary Problems," considers "the delineation of the appropriate boundary between the range of responsibilities for the decision of matters affecting individual and social welfare to be assigned to the individual decision-maker . . . and the range of responsibilities to be assigned to the state." Johnson does not agree with Friedman's position that institutional changes over the last two hundred years have left the relevancy of *The Wealth of Nations* unaffected. On the contrary, he argues that "the Smithian principles of free competition were developed against a particular historical background which has since been superceded as a consequence of processes of economic, political, and social change, and as a result there exists today a bias in favor of the interventionist position." Johnson concludes that arguments against the further growth of government must be couched in modern language and concepts, and offers as a possible line of approach quantitative economic tools such as cost-benefit analysis to evaluate "the relative efficiencies of government and of market decision-making." It was his pessimistic hope that government intervention into areas where it was less efficient than the market would be withdrawn.

Joseph Spengler, in his essay, "Smith Versus Hobbes: Economy Versus Polity," is also concerned with the appropriate roles of the state and the market. He, like Friedman, considers Smith's greatest contribution to be his vision of the market as a self-adjusting system based on the inherent desire of individuals to better their material condition, and that to this end the market is superior to the state. It thus followed in Smith's view that the role of the state should be severely curtailed in order that the market could operate in the optimal social order necessary to produce increased material well-being. Hobbes, on the other hand, argued that (in Spengler's words) "only a powerful apparatus of state can assure the order essential to a people's welfare, security, liberty, and conduct of human affairs." That Smith's paradigm, and not Hobbes', triumphed in the nineteenth century Spengler attributes to the industrial revolution, the alternative political means to the security of the individual put forth by Locke and others, and the growth of the middle class. In today's world, however, Spengler, like Johnson, believes that conditions are drastically different from those of two hundred years ago, and "as a result of ideological and ideational change the prevailing institutional structure no longer corresponds to one optimally compatible with an efficient free enterprise system." The danger of this condition, in Spengler's view, is that individuals are likely to be misled into believing that the Hobbesian solution will produce the more preferable social order.

James Buchanan's essay, "The Justice of Natural Liberty," is also concerned with the social order, but from the perspective of the institutional requirements necessary to insure justice. Specifically, Buchanan's purpose is to demonstrate that Adam Smith's "system of natural liberty" when applied to institutional reform in the contemporary American setting would produce essentially the same ordering of reform priorities that would result from the application of John Rawls' principle of "equal liberty." The difference between Smith and Rawls is shown by Buchanan to be that while *The Wealth of Nations* "concentrated on the efficiency-producing results of natural liberty [with] the corollary attributes of justice. . .not [being] stressed," Rawls on the other hand "treats liberty sketchily despite the lexical priority assigned to it, and he concentrates on the distributional qualities of an idealized social order." For both Smith and Rawls the basic institutional setting necessary for a just social order must be, according to Buchanan, that of an essentially free market economy.

Leonard Billet, in his essay, "Justice, Liberty and Economy," argues that Smith's fundamental concern was that of justice and how a society should be ordered so that justice should prevail. This central concern with justice begins in Smith's first book, *The Theory of Moral Sentiments,* and his ideas on human nature and the significance of justice in this work served as the basis for his views on political economy later put forward in *The Wealth of Nations.* Billet examines four aspects of Adam Smith's vision of the just economy: first, the moral justification of economic liberty; second, Smith's attitude towards labor and the laboring class; third, the role of government, and finally the anti-colonialism exposited in *The Wealth of Nations.*

The objective of William J. Baumol in his essay "Smith Versus Marx on Business Morality and the Social Interest" is to show that the differences in the treatment by Marx and Smith of the capitalist and the capitalist system derive from their views of man and history. For Smith, man is inherently selfish as a result of the Fall and it is the operation of the divine providence which has provided the market system to not merely curb human nature but "to put it to work for the common good." Marx, on the other hand, believed man to be prone towards neither good nor evil but that man's behavior is simply the result of historical circumstances. The capitalist just happened to be born at a stage in history when his role made him the exploiter of the working class. Baumol argues that to Smith's mind, eighteenth-century capitalism was simply a more complex form of the market economy which had existed from "the early and rude state of society." For Marx, however, capitalism was only a transitory stage of history preceding the final state of communism.

Ronald Max Hartwell, in his essay, "Adam Smith and the Industrial Revolution," considers two questions concerning Smith and the industrial revolution which have vexed historians of economic thought for many years. Specifically: (1) did Adam Smith realize that he was witnessing the beginning of what we now refer to as the industrial revolution?, and (2) what influence did Smith's ideas have in the making and sustaining of the industrial revolution? To answer the first question Hartwell examines five aspects of Smith's life: (a) his travel and observation, (b) his clubs and discussions, (c) his association with business men and politicians, (d) his library, and (e) his writings. Based on this evidence, Hartwell concludes that "Adam Smith was aware of the economic growth that was occurring in the eighteenth century, [and that] he was concerned primarily in *The Wealth of Nations* with explaining it in both economic and institutional terms." With respect to the second question, Hartwell considers the essence of Smith's policy prescription to be that of economic liberalism, and it was those nations in the nineteenth century that adopted policies based on Smith's vision that have had the greatest increase in material well-being.

In the concluding essay, "Adam Smith in Theory and Practice," Thomas Sowell evaluates the nature of the revolution touched off by the publication of *The Wealth of Nations,* compares it with other revolutions, and considers its present status. In order to accomplish this evaluation Sowell first presents the theory and practice of the system attacked by Smith—mercantilism—and then compares and contrasts this system with the theory and practice advocated by Smith— economic liberalism. In the fulfillment of this task Sowell provides us with a succinct summary of Smith's vision and justification for the title of founder of economic science that subsequent generations of economists have bestowed on Adam Smith.

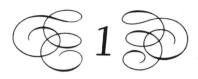

Adam Smith's Relevance for 1976

Milton Friedman
UNIVERSITY OF CHICAGO

H ISTORY never repeats itself." Yet "there is nothing new under the sun." 1976 is not 1776. Still, there are many resemblances that make Adam Smith even more immediately relevant today than he was at the Centennial of *The Wealth of Nations* in 1876.

Today, as in 1776, "by restraining, either by high duties, or by absolute prohibitions, the importation of such goods from foreign countries as can be produced at home, the monopoly of the home market is more or less secured to the domestic industry employed in producing them." (I, 418)[1] Today, to a far greater extent than in 1776, restrictions on foreign trade are reinforced by detailed interventions into domestic trade. Today, as then, government departs very far, indeed, from those elementary functions that Smith regarded as alone compatible with the "obvious and simple system of natural liberty."

Adam Smith was a radical and revolutionary in his time— just as those of us who preach laissez-faire are in our time. He was no apologist for merchants and manufacturers, or, more generally, for other special interests, but regarded them as the great obstacles to laissez-faire—just as we do today. He had no great confidence in his chances of success—any more than we can have today.

To expect, indeed, that the freedom of trade should ever be entirely restored in Great Britain, is as absurd as to expect that an Oceana or Utopia should ever be established in it. Not only the prejudices of the public, but what is much more unconquerable, the private interests of many individuals, irresistibly oppose it. Were the officers of the army to oppose with the same zeal and unanimity any reduction in the number of forces, with which master manufacturers set themselves against every law that is likely to increase the number of their rivals in the home market; were the former to animate their soldiers, in the same manner as the latter enflame their workmen, to attack with violence and outrage the proposers of such regulation; to attempt to reduce the army would be as dangerous as it has now become to attempt to diminish in any respect the monopoly which our manufacturers have obtained against us. This monopoly has so much increased the number of some particular tribes of them, that, like an overgrown standing army, they have become formidable to the government, and upon many occasions intimidate the legislature. The member of parliament who supports every proposal for strengthening this monopoly, is sure to acquire not only the reputation of understanding trade, but great popularity and influence with an order of men whose numbers and wealth render them of great importance. If he opposes them, on the contrary, and still more if he has authority enough to be able to thwart them, neither the most acknowledged probity, nor the highest rank, nor the greatest public services, can protect him from the most infamous abuse and detraction, from personal insults, nor sometimes from real danger, arising from the insolent outrage of furious and disappointed monopolists. (I, 435-36)

We are in a similar state today—except that we must broaden the "tribes" of "monopolists" to include not only enterprises protected from competition, but also trade unions, school teachers, welfare recipients, and so on and on.

Smith's pessimism turned out to be only partly justified. In 1846, seventy years after *The Wealth of Nations* appeared, the repeal of the Corn Laws in the United Kingdom ushered in a close approximation to that freedom of trade that he regarded as a dream. On the other side of the Atlantic, a comparable degree of freedom of international trade was never achieved, but an equal degree of freedom of internal trade was.

In the past century, we have come full circle. Throughout the world, the area of free trade—international and domestic— has declined. One restraint has been piled on another. Even where trade is freest, as within the massive United States economy, government today plays a far larger role than ever it did in Smith's time, let alone in the nineteenth-century high tide of laissez-faire.

Surely, the most cheerful message we could extract from Smith in this year 1976 is that we, too, may turn out to be wrong when we, too, fear that "to expect that the freedom of trade should ever be entirely restored" in the United States or Great Britain "is as absurd as to expect that an Oceana or Utopia should be established in it."

1. SPECIFIC ISSUES

Adam Smith is relevant to 1976 not only in the general sense just outlined, reflecting the turn of the wheel that has brought us back to an "overgoverned society," in Walter Lippman's phrase, but also in respect to highly specific issues of policy. I shall illustrate the extraordinary contemporaneity of *The Wealth of Nations* by examples from my own country, but I have no doubt that equally striking examples could be adduced by my fellow members for their own more than thirty countries.

1. We have recently been edified by the latest exhausting series of presidential primaries and the electoral campaign. Is there a better description of the participants' qualities, with their characteristic and simplistic preoccupation with short-term issues and tactics, than Smith's reference to "that insidious and crafty animal, vulgarly called a statesman or politician, whose counsels are directed by the momentary fluctuations of affairs?" (I, 432-33)

2. A major proposal of the Democratic party is the Humphrey-Hawkins bill, designed to "establish a process of long-range economic planning" which sets "a long-term full employment goal . . . at 3 percent adult unemployment, to be attained as promptly as possible, but within not more than 4 years after the date of the enactment of this Act," and which provides elaborate governmental machinery for these purposes.

Of the reams of print that have been spilled pro and con this bill and its immediate predecessor (the Humphrey-Javits bill),

none is more succinct and to the point than this comment
by Adam Smith:

The statesman, who should attempt to direct private people in what
manner they ought to employ their capitals, would not only load himself with a most unnecessary attention, but assume an authority which
could safely be trusted, not only to no single person, but to no council
or senate whatever, and which would nowhere be so dangerous as in the
hands of a man who had folly and presumption enough to fancy himself
fit to exercise it. (I, 421)

Has any contemporary political writer described Hubert
Humphrey more accurately, or devastatingly?

3. Or consider Smith's comment on the proposal by presidential candidate Ronald Reagan to decentralize government by
turning back functions and taxes from the federal government
to the states and cities:

The abuses which sometimes creep into the local and provincial administration of a local and provincial revenue, how enormous soever they may
appear, are in reality, however, almost always very trifling, in comparison
of those which commonly take place in the administration and expendi-
ture of the revenue of a great empire. They are, besides, much more
easily corrected. (II, 222)

4. Or weigh his comment on the effect of the growth of
government intervention into business in the form of I.C.C.,
F.C.C., F.T.C., Amtrak, Conrail, and so on.

Though the profusion of government must, undoubtedly, have retarded
the natural progress of [the United States[2]] towards wealth and improvement, it has not been able to stop it. (I, 327)
   The uniform, constant, and uninterrupted effort of every man to better
his condition, the principle from which public and national, as well as
private opulence is originally derived, is frequently powerful enough to
maintain the natural progress of things toward improvement, in spite
both of the extravagance of government, and of the greatest errors of
administration. (I, 325)

This comment is particularly relevant in light of the tendency
for enemies of freedom to attribute all defects in the world to
the market and all advances to beneficent state intervention.
As Smith stresses, improvements have come in spite, not
because, of governmental instrusion into the market place.

5. John Kenneth Galbraith, who has recently done a British Broadcasting Corporation television series on economists through the ages, has a very different view than I of Adam Smith's relevance today. He writes that "a sharp and obvious distinction must be made between what was important in 1776 and what is important now. The first is very great; the second, save in the imagination of those who misuse Smith as a prophet of reaction, is much less so. . . . Smith is not a prophet for our time." Perhaps this attitude is simply Galbraith's defensive reaction to Smith's devastating 1776 review of Galbraith's 1958 *Affluent Society,* with its stress on the contrast between private affluence and public squalor, and its denigration of "tail-fins" and other items of conspicuous consumption:

> It is the highest impertinence and presumption . . . in kings and ministers to pretend to watch over the economy of private people, and to restrain their expense, either by sumptuary laws, or by prohibiting the importation of foreign luxuries. They are themselves always, and without any exception, the greatest spendthrifts in the society. Let them look well after their own expense, and they may safely trust private people with theirs. If their own extravagance does not ruin the state, that of their subjects never will. (I, 328)

To which might be added Smith's devastating comment, "There is no art which one government sooner learns of another, than that of draining money from the pockets of the people." (II, 346)

6. As another example of Smith's relevance to specific issues, here is his comment on the widely proclaimed "social responsibility of business," and on those nauseating TV commercials that portray Exxon and its counterparts as in business primarily to preserve the environment: "I have never known much good done by those who affected to trade for the public good." He goes on to say (and here he was unduly optimistic): "It is an affectation, indeed, not very common among merchants, and very few words need be employed in dissuading them from it." (I, 421) Unfortunately, as George Stigler has often deplored, Adam Smith showed an uncharacteristic reticence at this point and never told us what those "few words" are.

7. It pains me to conclude this list of Smith's relevance to specific issues of 1976—but candor compels it—with two cases in which Smith provides arguments for the interventionist and statist, one minor, the other extremely important.

The minor case is Smith's defense of a legal maximum interest rate—which in part provoked Jeremy Bentham's subsequent splendid pamphlet, *In Defense of Usury*.

Smith is, of course, realistic about the limitations of such legislation, noting that where "interest of money has been prohibited by law . . . [it] has been found from experience to increase the evil of usury." (I, 338) Accordingly, he recommended that the legal maximum "rate ought always to be somewhat above the lowest market price, or the price which is commonly paid for the use of money by those who can give the most undoubted security." (I, 338) However, he goes on to say:

The legal rate . . . ought not to be much above the lowest market rate. If the legal rate of interest in Great Britain, for example, was fixed so high as eight or ten per cent, the greater part of the money which was to be lent, would be lent to prodigals and projectors who alone would be willing to give this high interest. Sober people, who will give for the use of money no more than a part of what they are likely to make by the use of it, would not venture into the competition. A great part of the capital of the country would thus be kept out of the hands which were most likely to make a profitable and advantageous use of it, and thrown into those which were most likely to waste and destroy it. (I, 338)

A highly uncharacteristic passage. Where here is that "highest impertinence and presumption" for which Smith elsewhere castigates ministers who "pretend to watch over the economy of private people"? Where is the faith earlier expressed in "the uniform, constant, and uninterrupted effort of every man to better his condition"? Where is the recognition that the usurer deserves the same description as he gives the smuggler, viz., "a person who, though no doubt highly blameable for violating the laws of his country, is frequently incapable of violating those of natural justice, and would have been, in every respect, an excellent citizen, had not the laws of his country made that a crime which nature never meant to be so"? (II, 381)

8. The major case in which Smith provided an argument that has since been used effectively by the statists and interventionists is in the key passage in which he describes the "three duties" that "the system of natural liberty" leaves the sovereign. The first two duties are unexceptionable: "first... protecting the society from the violence and invasion of other independent societies; secondly... protecting, as far as possible, every member of the society from the injustice or oppression of every other member of it, or... establishing an exact administration of justice." (II, 184-85)

The mischief is done by the third, "the duty of erecting and maintaining certain public works and certain public institutions, which it can never be for the interest of any individual, or small number of individuals, to erect and maintain; because the profit could never repay the expense to any individual or small number of individuals, though it may frequently do much more than repay it to a great society." (II, 185)

The third duty, which calls for relatively extended consideration, is mischievous because, on the one hand, properly interpreted, it does indicate a valid function of government; on the other hand, it can be used to justify a completely unlimited extension of government. The valid element is the argument for government intervention from third-party effects—or "external economies and diseconomies" in the technical lingo that has developed. If a person's actions impose costs or confer benefits on others, for which it is not feasible for him to compensate or charge them, then wholly voluntary exchange is not feasible; the third-party effects are involuntary exchanges imposed on other persons.

Smith's own statement of the "duty" is one-sided in two different respects. First, he considers only external economies, no external diseconomies. The currently popular pollution and environmental arguments can therefore not readily be included under his words, though his central point applies to them. Second, and far more important in my view, his statement does not allow for the external effects of the *governmental* actions in undertaking this duty, though, as we shall see, his discussion of particular government activities does do so. The major consideration that gives rise to significant third-party effects of private actions is the difficulty of identifying the external costs or benefits; if identification were relatively easy, it would be possible to subject them to voluntary exchange. But this same consideration hinders government actions, making it hard to evaluate the net effects of external costs and benefits and hard to avoid superimposing an additional set of external costs and benefits in taking supposedly corrective government action. In addition, governmental actions have further external effects, via their method of finance and via the danger to freedom from the expansion of government.

Perhaps the major intellectual fallacy in this area in the past century has been the double standard applied to the market and to political action. A market "defect"—whether through an absence of competition or external effects (equivalent, as recent literature has made clear, to transaction costs)—has been regarded as immediate justification for government intervention. But the political mechanism has its "defects," too. It is fallacious to compare the actual market with the "ideal" political structure. One should either compare the real with the real or the ideal with the ideal. Unfortunately, Smith's wording lends itself readily to this fallacy.

Smith himself spelled out at considerable length the "public works" and "public institutions" he included in his third duty. They were, first, those required to perform the first two duties of providing for defense and a system of justice. Second came those required "for facilitating the commerce of society," in which he included as "necessary for facilitating commerce in general," "good roads, bridges, navigable canals, harbours, etc." (II, 215) Though he recommended that the expense for these should, so far as possible, be defrayed by "tolls and other particular charges" (II, 215, marginal note), he did not regard the feasibility of so financing them as eliminating the argument for governmental rather than private construction. If a bridge or navigable canal is to be financed by specific charges why can it not be a private enterprise? Smith considers the question explicitly, notes that "canals are better in the hands of private persons than of commissioners" (II, 216-17, marginal note), but yet concluded, on what seem to me insufficient grounds, that "the tolls for the maintenance of a high road, cannot with any safety be made the property of private persons." (II, 217) Smith proceeded from those works and institutions for facilitating commerce in general to those for "facilitating particular branches of commerce." (II, 223) Here his main concern was with provision for protecting foreign trade, particularly with "barbarous" nations. But, as he expanded his analysis, the section turns into his famous attack on joint-stock companies.

The final major category of institutions which Smith included in his third duty were "the institutions for the education of youth." (II, 249) Here, again, he favored financing largely by specific fees. Despite Smith's acceptance of the appropriateness of governmental establishment and maintenance of such institutions, he devotes most of his discussion to a scathing attack on the effects of governmental or church control of institutions of learning—and his comments have a direct relevance today:

Those parts of education . . . for the teaching of which there are no public institutions, are generally the best taught. When a young man goes to a fencing or a dancing school, he does not indeed always learn to fence or to dance very well; but he seldom fails of learning to fence or to dance. (II, 253-54)

Today, try talking French with a graduate of public high school—or of a Berlitz school.

Were there no public institutions for education, no system, no science would be taught for which there was not some demand; or which the circumstances of the times did not render it either necessary, or convenient, or at least fashionable, to learn. (II, 266)

Despite his initial assertion that the erection of institutions for the education of youth is included in the third duty, these considerations lead him to ask, "Ought the public, therefore, to give no attention . . . to the education of the people?" (II, 267) He answers equivocally that in some cases it ought,

in others it need not. "In a civilized and commercial society,"
it is suggested, "the education of the common people requires
. . .the attention of the public more than that of people of
some rank and fortune." (II, 269) He concludes:

For a very small expense, the public can facilitate, can encourage, and can
even impose upon almost the whole body of the people, the necessity of
acquiring those most essential parts of education [to read, write, and
account]. The public can facilitate this acquisition by establishing in every
parish or district a little school, where children may be taught for a reward
so moderate, that even a common labourer may afford it; the master being
partly, but not wholly paid by the public; because, if he was wholly, or
even principally paid by it, he would soon learn to neglect his business.
(II, 270)

As this brief summary suggests, Smith himself did not regard
his third duty as providing extensive scope for governmental
activity. I do not criticize him for not recognizing its potential
for abuse. Though his prescience leads us to analyze *The Wealth
of Nations* as if it were a contemporary publication, he did
not have our experience but had to rely on his own. To
illustrate in a trivial way, could anyone write today as he did
then, "The post office. . .has been successfully managed by,
I believe, every sort of government"? (II, 303)

But since he wrote, there is hardly an activity which has not
been regarded as suitable for governmental intervention on
Smith's ground. It is easy to assert, as Smith himself does
again and again, that there are "external effects" which place
something or other in the "public interest" even though not
in the "interest of any individual or small number of individuals."
There are no widely accepted objective criteria by which to
evaluate such claims, to measure the magnitude of any external
effects, to identify the external effects of the governmental
actions, and to set them against the external effects of leaving
matters in private hands. Superficially scientific cost-benefit
analysis erected on Smith's basis has proved a veritable
Pandora's box.

2. GENERAL ISSUES

Beyond the particular issues just discussed, Smith's great
importance for 1976 and his great achievement—as Hayek and

others have so eloquently pointed out—is the doctrine of the "invisible hand," his vision of the way in which the voluntary actions of millions of individuals can be coordinated through a price system without central direction.

> As every individual, therefore, endeavours as much as he can both to employ his capital in the support of domestic industry, and so to direct that industry that its produce may be of the greatest value; every individual necessarily labours to render the annual revenue of the society as great as he can. He generally, indeed, neither intends to promote the public interest, nor knows how much he is promoting it . . . . He intends only his own gain, and he is in this, as in many other cases, led by an invisible hand to promote an end which was no part of his intention. Nor is it always the worse for the society that it was no part of it. By pursuing his own interest he frequently promotes that of the society more effectually than when he really intends to promote it. (I, 421)

This is a highly sophisticated and subtle insight. The market, with each individual going his own way, with no central authority setting social priorities, avoiding duplication, and coordinating activities, looks like chaos to untutored eyes. But through Smith's eyes we see that it is a finely ordered and effectively tuned system, one which arises out of men's individually motivated actions, yet is not deliberately created by men. It is a system which enables the dispersed knowledge and skill of millions of people to be coordinated for a common purpose. Men in Malaya who produce rubber, in Mexico who produce graphite, in the state of Washington who produce timber, and countless others, cooperate in the production of an ordinary rubber-tipped lead pencil—to use Leonard Read's vivid image—though there is no world government to which they all submit, no common language in which they could converse, and no knowledge of or interest in the purpose for which they cooperate.

Smith is often interpreted—and criticized—as the high priest of egotism and selfishness. That is very far from being the case. He was, first, a scientist who, driven by a sense of "wonder," excited by "incoherences" in the processes of the economy, sought "some chain of intermediate events, which, by connecting them with something that has gone before may render the whole course of the universe consistent and of a piece."[3] The subtle analysis of the price system was the result.

Second, on the moral level, Smith regarded sympathy as a pervasive human characteristic, but it was not unlimited and thus had to be economized. He would have argued that the invisible hand of the market was far more effective than the visible hand of government in mobilizing, not only material resources for immediate self-seeking ends, but also sympathy for unselfish charitable ends. And the nineteenth century is a dramatic vindication. In both the United States and the United Kingdom, much of that century comes about as close to Smith's system of natural liberty as it is reasonable to hope to achieve. And in both countries that century saw the greatest outpouring of eleemosynary and publicly directed activity that the world has ever seen. It was, in the United States, a century that produced a proliferation of private colleges and universities, of foreign missions, of nonprofit community hospitals, of the Society for the Prevention of Cruelty to Animals, of the non-government "public" library, of the Rockefeller and Carnegie Foundations, and so on and on. In Britain, the overwhelming bulk of hospital beds today are in hospitals constructed in the nineteenth century through voluntary action.

Though Smith fully develops the self-regulating market mechanisms only in *The Wealth of Nations,* in *The Theory of Moral Sentiments* he was already fully aware of the difference between an imposed order and what he would have called a natural order. In what is my own favorite Smith quotation, he gives a devastating critique of the modern well-intentioned interventionist who wants to attack major social problems via the political mechanism. Smith's name for him was "the man of system."

The man of system . . . seems to imagine that he can arrange the different members of a great society with as much ease as the hand arranges the different pieces upon a chess-board; he does not consider that the pieces upon the chess-board have no other principle of motion besides that which the hand impresses upon them; but that, in the great chess-board of human society, every single piece has a principle of motion of its own, altogether different from that which the legislature might choose to impress upon it. If those two principles coincide and act in the same direction, the game of human society will go on easily and harmoniously, and is very likely to be happy and successful. If they are opposite or different, the game will go on miserably, and the society must be at all times in the highest degree of disorder.[4]

The failure to understand this profound observation has produced an invisible hand in politics that is the precise reverse of the invisible hand in the market. In politics, men who intend only to promote the public interest, as they conceive it, are "led by an invisible hand to promote an end which was no part of their intention." They become the front men for special interests they would never knowingly serve. They end up sacrificing the public interest to the special interest, the interest of consumers to that of producers, the interest of the masses who never go to college to that of those who attend college, the interest of the poor working class saddled with employment taxes to that of the middle class who get disproportionate benefits from social security, and so on down the line.

The invisible hand in politics is as potent a force for harm as the invisible hand in economics is for good. At the moment, unfortunately, the former seems to have the upper hand. But the outlook is not entirely bleak. The far greater capacity of the many millions of ordinary men to find ways around government regulations, than of the fewer millions of bureaucrats to plug the leaks, provides some measure of freedom. The inefficiency of government arouses the resentment of the citizen, offers the chance of a tax revolt, and encourages a widespread anti-Washington sentiment. Perhaps it is not entirely chimerical to hope that our own corn laws will one day be overturned.

NOTES

1. All page references are to the Cannan edition of *An Inquiry into the Nature and Causes of the Wealth of Nations* (London: Methuen & Co. Ltd., 1930).
2. England in the original.

3. These words are from Smith's *History of Astronomy,* as quoted by W.P.D. Wightman, "Adam Smith and the History of Ideas," in *Essays on Adam Smith,* edited by Andrew S. Skinner and Thomas Wilson (Oxford: Clarendon Press, 1975), p. 50.

4. *The Theory of Moral Sentiments* (London: Henry G. Bohn, 1853), Arlington House 1969 reprint with Introduction by E.G. West, pp. 342-43.

The Individual and the State: Some Contemporary Problems

Harry G. Johnson
UNIVERSITY OF CHICAGO
GRADUATE INSTITUTE OF INTERNATIONAL STUDIES, GENEVA

THE bicentennial of the publication of Adam Smith's *The Wealth of Nations* provides both the stimulus and the opportunity for the re-examination of some of the fundamental themes with which Adam Smith—and following him the English classical school of economists—dealt in the book that established the specialized discipline of economics or, as it used to be known, "political economy."

Actually, the closer one approaches to the modern definition of "economics," the less of interest there is to be said about Adam Smith. For his two major "economics" subjects—the theory of the gains from free trade, and the principles of public finance—have become in pure theory exercises in the mathematics of distortions and the principles of "second-best," and in applied work applications of cost-benefit analysis by the economist in his role of servant to government planning; and his broad theme, the causes of the wealth of nations, has become translated into the naive specialist theory, sophisticated econometrics, and inventive applied statistics of central planning for economic development. So much the worse for economic science, many would say! Be that as it may—and the transmogrification of political economy into mathematical economics and econometrics is a theme I shall necessarily revert to later—it is the themes in the broader area of political economy that are the interesting ones to discuss, at least on an occasion such as this, and particularly the very broad question of the individual, the state, "liberty," and "the good society."

Before I address myself to this subject, however, I should make it perfectly clear that I have neither the scholarly knowledge nor the philosophical training necessary to discuss profoundly what Adam Smith himself had to say on these subjects, in *The Wealth of Nations* and its precursor, *The Theory of Moral Sentiments,* much as I could use more knowledge of his work and thoughts to illustrate what I propose to say. Rather, I take Adam Smith as a reference point for a tradition of political philosophy—the liberal philosophy—which extends backwards a long way into political philosophers such as Hobbes, Locke, and Rousseau, and forward through Herbert Spencer and contemporary liberal economist-philosophers such as Hayek, Buchanan, Tullock, and my colleague Milton Friedman. And I shall approach the questions I am concerned with far more as an intellectual than as a scholar of political economy, the difference being that an intellectual has heard about ideas that he can turn into interesting catch-phrases for scintillating discussion and titillating publications, while a scholar has thought about interesting ideas hard enough so that by the time he arrives at being able to explain the precise sense in which they are useful as well as interesting, he has lost most of his audience.

The question of the relation between the individual and the state, and specifically the delineation of the appropriate boundary between the range of responsibilities for the decision of matters affecting individual and social welfare to be assigned to the individual decision-maker (and more broadly, the voluntary processes of social decision-taking among social groups) on the one hand, and the range of responsibilities to be assigned to the state (or, more broadly, the ultimately coercive decision-taking processes of government) is a question that has become of growing importance in recent years. Ever since the process of rapid expansion of governmental responsibility for the welfare of the citizen-individual began—a process which can be identified roughly with the present century or the period since the first World War, though its origins can be traced back through the nineteenth century to Bentham as philosopher, Chadwick as social administrator, and John Stuart Mill as economist—there have of course been major exponents of the contrary view that the best society requires the assignment of the maximum possible responsibility (and liberty of choice) to the individual, and the minimum possible residual to the state. But the numbers and social importance of adherents to this view were reduced to virtual negligibility and social impotence by the combined effects of the great 1930s depression and the second World War, with Friedrich Hayek's *The Road to Serfdom* figuring as the last desperate act of heroic intellectual challenge to the forces of democratic centralism until the resurgence of conservatism (or true "radicalism" as Milton Friedman prefers to conceive it) in the 1960s. Moreover, "radicalism" of that type, like its opposite of "radicalism" as self-ascribed by various types of social criticism and stereotyped in the reporting of journalists, has been and remains a mini-minority taste, though often affected or patronized by conservatives and "practical" men. What has been the main motive force in raising the question of "the individual versus the state" has not been the propagation of a particular philosophy, but rather a questioning by the practical and pragmatic people of the not-all-that-quiet middle-class majority of the long-run social and economic effects of the development of the welfare state.

That questioning, in turn, can be related in very crude terms (in some ways paralleling the Marxist logic of inherent contradiction) to a type of idealized dynamics of the welfare state, as follows: A capitalist society with a built-in dynamics of growth and betterment of the lot of the average citizen, by its very success in that regard, generates both the assumption that the problem of production has been solved and that the problems of consumption and "the quality of life" are the important ones that should occupy social attention, and the belief that the economy and society can easily afford to redistribute a growing share of its automatically growing output from those who produce abundantly to those who do not, and from those who produce to those who supervise and administer collective consumption in the name of the society as a whole. The contradiction arises both because the abstraction of the resources required for these purposes directly diverts them from "productive" to "unproductive" uses—using the terms in the classical economics sense that distinguishes between activities that do and do not yield a surplus investible in accumulation and economic growth—and because the taxation required is progressively weighted against work and enterprise and in favor of what may be called the "rentier" or "landlord" approach to participation in the economic system. (I use the terms "rentier" and "landlord" for historical reasons. I could, in deference to the U.S. Bicentennial and this particular region of the United States, have referred instead to Veblen's theory of the leisure class; either terminology obviously fails completely to capture the essence of the contemporary phenomenon, which involves both the concept of a citizen's political right to consume regardless of productive contribution, and the general belief that having a large class of government employees whose function is to make choices for mere civilians for their own good is beneficial to everyone concerned, and indeed more beneficial to the pampered civilians than to the socially responsible civil servants.)

Concern about this inherent contradiction—which, unlike the Marxian one (or perhaps just like the Marxian one as history has refuted it), contains no logic of synthesis via revolution—has been aroused, rightly or wrongly, by the experience of world inflation and the unexpectedly deep depression of the last decade or less. One the one hand, inflation has been widely attributed, at least as a partial cause, to the demands of the welfare state pressing against the willingness of the taxpayers to bear the costs involved; while inflation itself has increased taxpayer resentment by its automatic effects in raising them into higher tax brackets as a consequence of tax brackets being defined in money terms. On the other hand, the set-back to economic growth and automatically increasing wealth resulting from depression and from the partial collapse of stock market prices and house values, and general uncertainty about the future, have made many practical people anxious about the prospective rising costs of the welfare state. This anxiety has had practical political expression in the loss of governmental power by "welfare-state" parties in Australia and in Sweden itself; and it has expressed itself also, perhaps to greater long-run effect, in the conventional financial journalists' treatment of the travails of the British economy as a horror-story of what is likely to happen in the United States if present trends continue.

There is, I think, a real problem to worry about: how to reconcile the achievement of the worthy aims of the welfare state, or more narrowly the provision of social security, with the preservation of the values of individual initiative and responsibility, and at the same time to avoid the transformation of our society into one dominated by the combination of a vast bureaucracy and a high proportion of unproductive or insuffiently productive consumers. Both impose an onerous burden on the self-reliant producer-consumer which he will have a growing incentive to escape by changing his economic class and joining one of the other two groups, according to his talents and opportunities. Fundamentally, this problem is a combination of three basic problems in political economy that the classical economists wrestled with. These were the physiocrats' problem of excessive taxation of the produce of the land, the source of the social surplus above subsistence; Adam Smith's problem of government interference with the pursuit of individual self-interest (though Smith was more concerned with the legislators than with the bureaucrats of his day); and the problem of unproductive consumption of rent by the landlord, on which the classical economists were divided but which they did not treat as central. (Later, however, in the hands of Marx, Christian doubts about the moral claim of the landlord to his rents from landed property were transformed into moral certainty of the lack of entitlement of the capitalist to the profits from his accumulation of material capital, a moral judgment given pseudo-scientific status by the assertion that the worker ought to receive the total product but is "exploited," and the inference that since the competitive capitalist system forces the capitalist to accumulate he deserves no credit for sacrificing present consumption in order to do so.)

The problem, and its antecedents in classical economics, is easy enough to recognize. The difficulty is to translate it into terms that make sense to contemporary thinkers about the social system and its economic organization. The appeal to the notion of "freedom" and "the free society," voiced less or more stridently by thinkers ranging from Hayek and Friedman to Ayn Rand, seems largely mystical and even neurotic or even paranoid to the ordinary educated man, most excusably inter-pretable as a throwback to the inter-war European experience of rivalry between communism and fascism for inheritance of the anti-democratic tradition of the national-imperial state. The efforts of others, such as Buchanan and Tullock, and Breton and Scott, who have been attempting to build on and modernize the pre-modern but post-divine-monarchical-state concept of the "social contract," seem intolerably artificial. In fact, they are artificial since they assume that the individual materializes from nowhere in a fully adult, civilized and socialized condition. More importantly, these efforts are completely unrealistic since they must implicitly throw the responsibility for socialization on the institution of the family, which for this purpose must be idealized beyond recognition or reasonableness. (I have never forgotten an interchange between a socialist English sociologist I know, and Milton Friedman, which ended with the sociologist saying: "Milton, at last I've understood the difference between us: you believe in the family, and I don't!") For the practical man, also, the idea of self-reliance is attractive, but not to the point of willing-ness to forswear the social help that judicious government intervention might give him; and the concept and presumed character of government as depicted by at least the more logically consistent of present-day disciples of Adam Smith is utterly alien to everyday experience. In consequence, the radical free enterprisers are only too vulnerable to the charge that they are vainly trying to turn the hands of the clock back to a bygone historical era.

To put the same point in another and more positive way, the Smithian principles of free competition were developed against a particular historical background which has since been superceded as a consequence of processes of economic, political, and social change. To put the relevant considerations briefly, Britain in Smith's time was governed, not by democracy, but by a landed aristocracy. The mercantilism Smith attacked was a policy designed to appeal to legislators ignorant and indeed disdainful of commerce, for the benefit of the merchant classes, who themselves lacked independent political power. The jobs provided in doing the government's administrative work and managing its finances were filled on the patronage system, and often contracted and subcontracted out again: "public service" was either loyal service to the ruling class, or self-service, or both together. Most important, economic activity was based on rather simple, or if not simple, traditionally familiar, technologies that were within the grasp of the man of average intelligence and education. Adam Smith's celebrated pin factory, with its to-him-impressive specialization and division of labor and use of machinery, would today be one of the stigmata of a developing country of the third or even fourth world.

Since that time, and since the half-to-full century thereafter during which the main lines of both conservative and liberal (in the American sense, "radical" in the popular sense) positions with respect to the capitalist or free enterprise system were worked out, the Smithian world has been changed beyond recognition, and in ways that are strongly and pervasively biased against the Smithian tradition and in favor of the interventionist position.

In the first place, the aristocratic form of government has been transformed through the extension of the franchise to include the unpropertied, the females, and those under the age of full responsible adulthood and parenthood, into the contemporary democratic form. In consequence, government can no longer be conceived of as a juxtaposition of myself, the citizen-subject, against them, the rulers of my nation. Instead, government and its works and responsibilities are an aspect of myself and my works and responsibilities. The relation between the individual and the state is not a matter of balancing my obligations to others against my own freedom, but of a choice or allocation of responsibilities between two methods of serving my own interests: private or individual, and public or collective choice and responsibility.

Second, and particularly important with the subsequent rapid and large-scale expansion of governmental activity, the basis for recruitment to the public service has been shifted from the patronage system to selection based on educational attainment and competitive examination. This in turn has meant the virtual disappearance of any social distinction between government and private employment and advancement, especially as the differential advantage of the public service in terms of security of tenure has been undermined by the growth of corporate enterprises affording comparable security of tenure, and by the safety of most private-sector employment provided through the combination of government commitment to the maintenance of high employment, generous social security arrangements, and the seniority rules established by collective bargaining. Not only does the legislative branch of government legislate in my name and on my behalf, but the administrative branch administers the legislation on my behalf by employing people just like me. If anything, these people are better educated and informed about my problems than I myself, and therefore better able to cope with them than I am. More accurately, while I may arrogantly dispute this proposition in my own particular case, in some contexts, I am inclined to believe it to be generally true for the mass of my fellow-citizens. The individual in the contemporary state, in other words, has no presumption that government choices and administrative decisions are inherently and necessarily worse than private choices and decisions would be; in fact, he is strongly inclined, for reasons to be discussed shortly, to make the opposite presumption.

Third, the processes of discovery of new scientific knowledge and its application through invention, innovation, distribution, and marketing have required and fostered the development of the non-family-controlled, competitively staff-and-management-recruiting, limited liability corporation. The corporation in its internal activities is organized in a non-market, bureaucracy-like fashion, with decision-taking by committee and consensus procedures, with internal competition being subject to political and social rather than direct competitive-market-profit tests of efficiency. One consequence is that there has been considerable controversy among economists specializing in industrial organization over what if anything the corporation seeks to maximize, and whether the forces of competition and the mechanisms of the market in fact discipline the internal organization into pursuit of profit-maximization on theoretical atomistic-competitive lines in its external aspect in spite of institutional appearances to the contrary. More relevant to the present argument, corporate economic success requires the same sort of use of cooperation among people of diverse backgrounds with the abilities of qualified (and in a sense dispassionate and objective) professional experts as does government itself. In short, government is not basically a different kind of activity, employing different principles of organization, than private economic activity. It is the same kind of activity, organized on the same operating principles, as private corporate enterprise. It differs only in the character of the shareholders to whom it is responsible, the means by which they acquire their shares, the market in which it sells its product, and the currency in which it measures its profits or losses. Consequently, the man who has made a successful career in the private sector has no real problem in changing to a career in the public sector

(or for that matter, vice versa). More important, he has no
reason not to espouse governmental or private sector solutions
to problems he regards as social, or as involving business or
business activities other than those in which he is directly,
personally involved.

Two other related characteristics of contemporary economic
life should be mentioned. First, the expertise required for
higher-level participation in the corporate private enterprise
sector is attained through formal education in secondary and
vocational schools and universities. These institutions are themselves non-market institutions, and their teaching staff and
general atmosphere tend to be permeated by belief in governmental methods of (at least social) problem-solving. By this
I mean belief in the process of committee and consensus
decision-taking by deliberation and judgment, among at least
nominally dispassionate people of superior training. This is
quite apart from the familiar observation that the staffs of
educational institutions tend to be self-selected from among
those who for one reason or another dislike subjecting themselves to open-market competition, and the less familiar
observation that those who teach in primary and secondary
schools tend to gravitate into those jobs as a result of mediocre
or poor academic performance at a higher educational level,
and frequently bear considerable latent or overt resentment
against "the capitalist system," to whose reliance on
performance rather than character they attribute their own
relative lack of worldly success. Second, the expansion of the
government sector, in conjunction with the successful insistence
that public servants should have the same rights of political
participation as privately-employed citizens, means a quantitatively important group of voters who are committed almost
automatically to the use and extention of the governmental
rather than the private-enterprise variety of problem-solving.
(I say "almost automatically," because I once met an official
of the British Board of Trade—the equivalent of our Department of Commerce—who claimed and believed himself, with
some justification, to be a firm adherent of the policy of

freedom of international trade, but even he believed that an exception should be made for policies designed to increase Britain's ability to export high-technology industrial products.)

Fourth and finally, among the changes in the socio-economic conjuncture that have occurred since Adam Smith's time, there has been both the "narrowing down" of the family from an extended kinship unit spanning different generations and many children—both siblings and their cousins—to the nuclear, typically two-parent two-child, family unit, and the raising of social standards regarding the content and results of bringing up children. The growing gap between what parents can actually do and what society expects them to do for their children has been increasingly filled by the school-teaching professions on the one hand and the social workers' professions on the other—which means the replacement of individual private by collective public decision-taking with respect to the main aims of childhood learning experience, and accustoming the child to external governmental group decision rather than internal family group or individual decision.

The shift from family to social/governmental decision-taking with respect to children's education has been reinforced by a number of factors, of which one worthy of special note is the fact that life in an economy of extreme specialization and division of labor, in which high income frequently depends on some arcane technical or executive skill, makes parents unable to teach their children much if anything about the way the economy in which they will eventually participate actually works. In important ways the modern economy, at least as it appears to the child, closely resembles the land-based feudal economic system: the family's standard of living seems to be provided automatically, by some mysterious property right the father has established in the outside world, which requires his spending part of his time out there doing something or other of an incommunicable nature, after which he comes home to spend his spare time doing nothing much, or nothing that his children (as they grow past infancy) cannot do at least as well as he can; and typically he knows far less about the things they study in school than they and their classmates do, let alone their teachers. The parents', and particularly the fathers', authority seems to rest on the arbitrary possession of power—initially the power of adult size and strength, later the power of financial control over the intra-family allocation of the family's freely disposable income. It is not surprising that the process of maturation into adulthood should entail inter-generational conflict over finance that in a significant minority of cases is transferred into a "radical" view of the nature of the capitalist system and a corresponding protest against it, or into the assumption that the problem of social justice is one of fair distribution of the surplus above the unrecognized cost of maintaining the accustomed standard of living. More generally and pervasively, the modern family unit transmits little if any information about the processes of market competition; instead, it typically provides many cushions against the implications and consequences of exposure to it. It provides a great deal of indoctrination in the belief that society could and should be better organized for the family's benefit by extension of non-market, or governmental, methods of control.

The consequence of all these factors is, as already mentioned, that contemporary society generates many biases towards belief in the superiority of governmental control and decision-taking over market organization and decision-taking. Moreover, the consequence of these biases is a cumulative trend towards increasing the role of government, because, in contrast to the assumption traditional to both political theory and political economy, people do not arrive simultaneously in society as self-sufficient, self-determining adults capable of making and enforcing a once-and-for-all social contract determining the division between private and social responsibilities, but are born serially and grow within an existing social framework that strongly conditions their ideas of what the framework itself should be and what the directions of change should be. Thus arguments against the further extension of government, and in favor of a return towards greater reliance on private initiative and decision-making, are not only demanding the reversal of a strong and many-faceted social trend, but insofar as they are couched in terms of the language and concepts used in discussing the problem as it appeared in some past period, are likely to be ineffective or even counter-effective, because they are only too easily dismissable as archaic, irrelevant, and even hysterically emotional and irrational.

The problem that this points to, for those who are seriously concerned about the classic problem of the relation between the individual and the state to which Adam Smith provided what seemed for over a century of economic development to be the definitive answer, is how to reformulate the problem in a contemporarily relevant and intellectually exciting way. How can this be done? My short answer is that I do not know (if I did, I would be speaking on that subject instead of the present one, presumably to a quite different audience). My longer answer is that contemporary economics suggests an approach that might be as effective as classical political economy was. It would require a reliance on economic science rather than on stereotyped assumptions about the nature of government and of the individual in relation to society. It would have to enlist the belief of public opinion in the scientific approach which currently provides uncritical support for the general presumption that the governmental decision-making process is superior to the competitive market process because it makes more explicit and comprehensive use of expert scientific knowledge. The approach I have in mind is simple to describe though obviously difficult to carry out: to apply quantitative economic methods, on cost-benefit and cost-effectiveness lines, to the question of the relative efficiencies of government and of market decision-making processes in various areas of decision-taking. A start, but only a start, has been made by my colleague George J. Stigler, in his researches on the effects, if any, of efforts to improve the working of markets by government regulations and regulating agencies. The main problem of such a scientific exercise, as I see it, is not technical but motivational: those who favor the individual will be too easily satisfied with evidence against government, and too ready to explain away evidence in its favor. On the other hand, those who favor the government will be unlikely to raise the question at all, or consider the question worth studying at all—unless the evidence is strongly enough adverse to government to warrant the attempt to demolish the scientific qualifications of those who produce it. This is perhaps an excessively pessimistic view; unfortunately, it rests on a fair amount of empirical evidence of the behavior of our profession when it is confronted by a genuine problem in political economy.

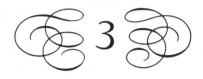

Smith Versus Hobbes: Economy Versus Polity

Joseph J. Spengler

DUKE UNIVERSITY

It is a living proof of the aberrations of which a scholarly group is capable when it does not have the good fortune to find serious opponents.   Carl Menger, *Untersuchungen*

But though empires, like all the other works of men, have all hitherto proved mortal, yet every empire aims at immortality.   Adam Smith, W.N., Bk. 5, chap. 2*

1. INTRODUCTION

OVER time every society has developed two sets of apparatus or institutions, *economy* or *market economy* and *state* or *polity,* to each of which direction of large portions of its essential functions has gravitated. Over the centuries these two sets have interacted and the distribution of essential functions between them has fluctuated. For essential functions have increased and their character has changed; political power has been redistributed, technology and facilities have improved,

---

* For convenience in the text I use the initials W.N., M.S., L, and E, respectively, to identify Adam Smith's *The Wealth of Nations* (Modern Library), *The Theory of Moral Sentiments,* 1853 (Bohn's Standard Library), *Lectures on Justice, Police, Revenue, and Arms* (New York: Kelley, 1956) and *The Essays of Adam Smith* (London: Murray, 1872).

and organizations alternative to both the market as such and the state have come into being.[1] The fundamental purpose of the state has always been recognized as the avoidance of anarchy and political chaos, together with the maintenance of order through recourse to whatever instruments of coercion are required. The fundamental purpose of the economy, defined in terms of the specialized production and exchange of goods and services, has been the supply of man's material needs and desires, mainly through recourse to activities entailing a balance of rewards over costs to the organizations and agencies constituting the economy.

Whereas the apparatus of state is operated coercively from an overall command post, together with diverse satellite command posts, a market economy functions as a self-adjusting mechanism made up of numerous lesser self-adjusting mechanisms which, singly and as a totality, respond to changes internal and/or external to the market economy when it pays decision-makers so to respond. Furthermore, whereas the state apparatus is supported mainly by critical inputs originating in the economy, the latter is required to sustain both itself and the state, even when the state takes over functions better performed within the economy and by its apparatus.

As these two sets of institutions, *polity* and *economy* (especially in its market form) have evolved and interacted, so have the visions or models which philosophers and scholars have formed of them in order to understand the role and operation of each. Both polity and economy have had favorable spokesmen over the centuries. However, polity has commanded more attention because it has always been more visible and easier to perceive as an operating, directed entity than is an economy in the shape of a self-adjusting system of self-adjusting actors. Moreover, because a polity is visible and leaves more easily identifiable tracks than an economy, scholars, too often more responsive to available data than to the phenomenology of events and issues of significance, have exaggerated the role of the state.[2] In the annals of man his servitors and the poor have commanded much less attention than the exploiting few.

"History," Henri Fabre has said, "celebrates the battlefields whereon we meet our death, but scorns to speak of the plowed fields whereby we thrive."[3]

This year we celebrate the bicentennial of *The Wealth of Nations,* greatest of man's economic works and devoted to exposition of the superiority of a free economy to a polity in respect of its capacity to meet man's material needs and thus make his aesthetic, philosophical, and spiritual desires more satisfiable. With Smith's system, a product of evolution as was English common law, we shall contrast Hobbes' system which is describable as in the tradition of Seneca and the Christian Fathers who, contrary to Aristotle and Cicero, found in private property and the state coercive institutions essential to making earthly life tolerable in the face of mankind's wickedness, an "ethical second-best" as the great political scientist, George Sabine, put it.[4] Hobbes did not, of course, anticipate the emergence of the modern Orwellian totalitarian state, equipped with a powerful bureaucracy armed with modern techniques of communication and control and resting on rootless, malleable mass man.[5] Had he done so he would have repudiated it.

2. ANTICIPATIONS

While Hobbes' model was conjectural rather than historical, many explanations of the origins of government run in parallel terms, namely, that in the absence of a strong government political chaos prevails, solution for which consists in a form of social contract or some other basis on which absolutist rulership may rest should ordination of the ruler not lie immediately with God. Illustrative instances are found in Indian political thought,[6] and in the works of the Chinese Legalist School.[7] Greek philosophers noted how justice favored the stronger, or could be thought of as anarchy-preventing convention. Herodotus reports how the Medes agreed to set a king over them and be "well governed , . . . able to attend to our own affairs, and not be forced to quit our country on account of anarchy."[8] In the *Laws* (I, p. 626) Plato has Cleinias speak for the Cretan lawgiver: "For what men in general term peace would be said by him to be only a name; in reality every city is in a natural state of war with every other, not indeed proclaimed by heralds, but everlasting." Thucydides (whose work Hobbes himself translated) described the early Greeks as living under stark conditions and "the richest soils" as "always most subject to . . . change of masters."[9]

Whereas convention and plan rather than Austinian logic or evolution underlay models of polities of which Hobbes' polity is an examplar, Smith's economy, together with its compatible polity counterpart, was an outcome of what Carl Menger in 1883 called organic growth as manifested in the development of man's economic institutions (e.g., money, property, state, etc.).[10] Menger's view may reflect the evolution-oriented outlook of the nineteenth century, especially when contrasted with the dominantly reformist, planning orientation of eighteenth-and twentieth-century ideology and ideation.

Inasmuch as exchange has always been the central focus of economics it is in the history of exchange and man's study of it that we must seek the impact of the climate of opinion that underlay the origin and growth of the thought of Adam Smith. Exchange is a positive-sum game and has usually been viewed as such. For exchange, together with the accompanying bargaining process, facilitates commercial contact, eliminates differences in interests, and augments the utility derivable from the goods and services subject to voluntary, non-coercive exchange. Free exchange serves to bind people together within communities and to draw together members of neighboring and even distant communities.[11]

The growth and extent of exchange testifies to growing awareness of its utility and adaptability, whether it be complex or the "silent" trade described by Pliny and Herodotus.[12] Trade was extensive in the Mediterranean world as in Mesopotamia, West Asia, India, and China long before the Christian Era. In the Middle East, for example, already in the third millenium B.C. we find economically oriented organization, media of exchange and banking, writing, record-keeping, and regulations essential to the conduct of transactions subject to consummation over time.[13]

The Graeco-Roman world, writes Finley, was "essentially and precisely one of private ownership" whereas "the Near Eastern economies were dominated by large palace-or temple-complexes, who owned the greater part of the arable, virtually monopolized anything that can be called 'industrial production' as well as foreign trade (which includes inter-city trade, not merely trade with foreign ports), and organized the economic, military, political, and religious life of the society through a single complicated, bureaucratic, record-keeping operation for which the word 'rationing,' taken very broadly, is [a] one-word description."[14] Finley probably overstates the degree to which "rationing" characterized Near Eastern economies since some of these evolved into mixed economies. Finley's description not only fits the Roman world quite well until the demoralization that preceded the accession of Diocletian but also reflects the influence of Cicero who, long before Locke, identified the "twofold conception of order and freedom (*imperium et libertas*)" with "the rights of property."[15] Unfortunately, the evils of bureaucratization were intensified by the crowding of lawyers into the ranks of the civil hierarchy where they became "one of the chief plagues of contemporary society."[16] It was not until in the second millenium, after a slow and protracted recovery from Rome's collapse, that trade picked up over a wide area in Europe.[17]

Because of its importance to community cohesion and economic welfare, philosophers and legists were concerned that exchange be so carried on as to assure its continuity. One might, as did some lawmakers (e.g., Hammurabi),[18] prohibit individual types of injustice, or set down preconditions to justice as Plato, Aristotle, Cicero, and others attempted to do, or derive rules from a supposed Natural Order, or (as Greek "liberals" preferred) arrive at rules experimentally, or count upon a competitive price system to keep exchange "just."[19] Of overriding importance is the Greek conception of justice as the bond of men in states, and of the functions of justice in exchange, and of distributive justice, particularly as formulated by Aristotle,[20] and subsequently introduced into Roman legal thought, mainly by Cicero, and thence into the Christian conception of justice. In the *Institutes of Justinian* justice is defined as "the set and constant purpose which gives to every man his due," and "the precepts of law" are given as "to live honestly, to injure no one, and to give every man his due."[21] To all this "just price," as formulated in the West,[22] was a sequel, though not unique in principle since one finds a formal equivalent to just price in Mesopotamian, Indian, and Chinese 'economic' or legal literature.

The distinguished Roman lawyer, Rudolph Sohm, in his *The Institutes,* put what has been said as follows:

Law, in the juristic sense . . . embodies that ordered control of the life of a people which is necessary for the preservation of a people and which, for that very reason, is morally binding on the individual. It regulates the relations of power within a people in accordance with the ideal of justice which resides in the community of that people, and the ultimate source of which is the belief in divine justice.

Justice is a principle regulating the distribution of things valued by men—awarding them to some, denying them to others—and it is, at the same time, a principle whereby man's worth is appraised. Justice gives to "everyone that which is his," that which (in other words) is due to him according to his worth.

He adds,

All law exists in order that the people may live and be strong, and the power of law over the individual is rooted in that subordination of individual life to the common life which is demanded by morality. The people claim back from the individual the life which it gave him. Populum vivere necesse est, te vivere non necesse est. Law apportions to each individual that which is due to him as a member of the people, and due to him, moreover, for the sake of the people. Herein lies the true significance of the suum cuique, in its legal sense.[23]

3. STATE VERSUS MARKET: SMITH

In theory justice may flourish either under the aegis of an ideal state or under a free economy buttressed in a minor degree by collectivist supplementation when pronounced externalities are involved. In reality, however, the apparatus of state serves best those who control it whereas in a market-dominated society there tends to be a high degree of correspondence between reward and performance. Such in essence seems to have been Smith's view. Of overriding importance in Smith's assessment, however, is this: the market is self-adjusting, its lesser components are self-adjusting, and the individual is comparatively free of external constraint upon his moving from where he is to what appear to be preferable situations.

Smith thus spoke for the great superiority of a self-adjusting system to its alternatives—for a system composed of numerous self-adjusting decision makers animated by self-interest and capable of serving both man's material needs and indirectly many of his less material desires. Smith's emphasis is both upon the stabilizing, self-adjusting character of this system and upon the comparative limitedness of the residual role of the state under normal conditions, though it could be elastic in the presence of temporary expansion of collective needs.[24]

To Smith's equilibrating economic system there necessarily corresponded a limited political order, an order stable and optimal when the state confined its activities to areas in which it enjoyed a comparative advantage and eschewed the pork-barrel role dominant today.

Smith's system, analogues of which are perceivable in Locke, Cantillon, Quesnay, and Hume, emerged not only out of a general awareness of the advantages associated with free exchange but also out of what his modern predecessors had written in response to their perception of these advantages. For, as Letwin observes, "All the efforts of seventeenth- and eighteenth-century economic writers culminated in *The Wealth of Nations;* everything useful that they did, Adam Smith incorporated; everything worth doing that they left undone, he accomplished. His was the achievement and yet it was his partly because luck placed him at that moment in the development of a tradition when all the materials lay ready to his hand."[25] Smith's *The Wealth of Nations,* continues Letwin, "deserves its reputation, not as in any way an ultimate statement, but as a turning point, the beginning of all that came after as it was the end of all that came before."[26]

To this I would add that it is the essentially self-adjusting character of Smith's system that is so fundamental, not a

completely mechanical system such as an engineer or physicist
contrives, but one that allows for human quirks, inconsistencies, Homeric nods, misinterpretations, poor information flow,
the supra-incremental as well as the incremental, enough
individuality to dissipate mass-response—in sum, enough
adjustability to permit the system to absorb changes in options
and, as H. A. Simon might put it, "satisfice"[27] enough
individuals to insure political and economic stability so long as
most individuals are free to act in their self-interest.

It was the threat of the rise of the regulative state that Smith
popularized, living as he did in an age that perceived order in
seeming chaos and economic behavior in keeping with the
requisites of a self-maintaining and stabilizing economic
order.[28] Smith put it this way:

All systems either of preference or of restraint, therefore, being thus
completely taken away, the obvious and simple system of natural liberty
establishes itself of its own accord. Every man, as long as he does not
violate the laws of justice, is left perfectly free to pursue his own interest
his own way, and to bring both his industry and capital into competition
with those of any other man, or order of men. The sovereign is completely
discharged from a duty, in the attempting to perform which he must
always be exposed to innumerable delusions, and for the proper
performance of which no human wisdom or knowledge could ever be
sufficient; the duty of superintending the industry of private people, and
of directing it towards the employments most suitable to the interest
of the society. (WN, p. 651)

Smith, while never guilty of the "Fallacy of Misplaced
Concreteness,"[29] several times used the unseen hand metaphor
to illustrate how the pursuit of private interest, in the absence
of state intervention on its behalf, brings about socially salutary
albeit unintended results. (MS, pp. 264-65; WN, p. 423)

As every individual, therefore, endeavors as much as he can both to
employ his capital in the support of domestic industry, and so to direct
that industry that its produce may be of the greatest value; every
individual necessarily labours to render the annual revenue of the society
as great as he can. He generally, indeed, neither intends to promote the
public interest, nor knows how much he is promoting it . . . . [A]nd by
directing that industry in such a manner as its produce may be of the
greatest value, he intends only his own gain, and he is in this, as in many

other cases, led by an invisible hand to promote an end which was no
part of his intention. Nor is it always the worse for the society that it was
no part of it. (WN, p. 423)

Smith's invisible-hand metaphor may have been inspired by
Joseph Glanvill (1636-1680) who held that "the most common
Phaenomena can be neither known, nor improved without
Insight into the more *hidden* frame. For *Nature* works by an
Invisible Hand in all things"—a hand that Fontenelle, in his
Pluralité des Mondes (1686), a work known to Smith, compared
to that of the Engineer who, hidden in the pit of a French
Theatre, operated "the Machines of the Theatre" in motion
on the stage.[30] This metaphor, of origin in the seventeenth
century, the "Century of Genius" according to Whitehead,[31]
together with its use, reflects what Whitehead calls in another
connection "a widespread instinctive conviction in the existence
of an *Order of Things,* and, in particular, of an *Order of Nature*"
despite the fact that "nothing ever really recurs in exact detail."
The men of Smith's "century rationalised the social life of
modern communities, and based their sociological theories on
an appeal to the facts of nature."[32]

Philosophy, according to Smith, revealed the order underlying seeming chaos. "Philosophy, by representing the invisible
chains which bind together all these disjointed objects,
endeavours to introduce order into this chaos of jarring and
discordant appearances, to allay this tumult of the imagination,
and to restore it, when it surveys the great revolutions of the
universe, to that tone of tranquility and composure, which is
both most agreeable in itself and most suitable to its nature"
(E, p. 335; also p. 392). Though fully aware of the utility of
conceptualizing and systematizing interrelated phenomena,
Smith avoided what Whitehead called the fallacy of misplaced
concreteness, nemesis of the model builder. "All philosophical
systems," Smith remarked respecting Newton's "system" are
"mere inventions of the imagination" designed to connect
"otherwise discordant and disconnected phenomena of Nature"
in the "imagination" (E, p. 384); and, when discussing moral
philosophical systems, Smith warned that reducing a set of

moral doctrines "into a scholastic or technical system" was "one of the most effectual expedients, perhaps, for extinguishing whatever degree of good sense there may be in any moral or metaphysical doctrine." (MS, p. 425-26)

Smith was no Candide, no endorser of Leibniz's "optimism" (*Theodicy,* 1710). Instead he stressed the importance of guarding the system of natural liberty and the world of competition against subversive forces. He indicated the need for "general rules of morality" born of experience and for "sacred laws of justice" to govern "self-love" and competitive behavior. (MS, pp. 120-21, 224-28, 249-51) Smith apparently believed, however, that if the apparatus of state was not mobilized in support of these subversive forces, the inherent strength of the natural system of liberty would dissipate them. For in his day it was virtually impossible for great economic power to be concentrated in the absence of state support.[33]

Smith did not touch upon justice in the classical-scholastic tradition in *The Wealth of Nations,* presumably because in a system of liberty justice in exchange would result and freedom made it easier for the individual to improve his relative as well as his absolute condition. In his *Moral Sentiments,* however, Smith touched upon both commutative and distributive justice (MS, pp. 397-402), but he noted that no rules embodying the principles of these two types of justice had been laid down (MS, pp. 502-3). Moreover, none of the systems of moral philosophy described by him incorporated a corrective feedback system as did the system of natural liberty.

Systems of positive law could "never be regarded as accurate systems of the rules of natural justice" even though rules were necessary and intended when enunciated "to coincide with those of natural justice." (MS, p. 502) Because one man will not submit to violation of justice from another, "the public magistrate is under necessity of employing the power of the commonwealth to enforce the practice of this virtue" (i.e., justice). Then, Smith continues in terms remindful of Hobbes, "without this precaution, civil society would become a scene of bloodshed and disorder, every man revenging himself at his own hand whenever he fancied he was injured. To prevent the confusion which would attend upon every man's doing justice to himself, the magistrates, in all governments that have acquired any considerable authority, undertake to do justice to all, and promise to hear and redress every complaint of injury" in keeping with prescribed rules. (MS, pp. 501-2)

4. STATE VERSUS MARKET: HOBBES

Thomas Hobbes (1588-1679) is not so important in himself as in his description of a societal organization at the opposite pole from Smith's and currently in the process of superseding Smith's albeit in forms similar in spirit rather than in detail to Hobbes' system. Hobbes did not, of course, consider systems anticipatory of Smith though he had less confidence in juristic law as such than did Roman-Law jurists who believed that it made the individual morally free and allowed private law to transform men into communities of free individuals and thus make possible a free economy of the sort Adam Smith contemplated. For, unlike primitive law which rested on the view that the gods punished what was wrong and shielded what was right, juristic law could and did allow many of the sanctions contributive to economically productive behavior to be incorporated in the market.[34] Hobbes feared, however, that man's inability to triumph over scarcity would not permit so salutary an outcome.

Hobbes' lack of confidence rested upon his interpretation of man's capacity to achieve stability in a world of scarcity—a world that he envisioned hypothetically if not empirically even as did Hume, Malthus, and others later. However, Hobbes' critics, Locke, Quesnay, Smith, and others, believed nature to be a potential source of abundance requiring only human freedom and democratic institutions to be realized.[35] Hume argued in effect, Commons suggests, that "justice and Private Property arise from *relative scarcity*. But communism . . . arises from *total scarcity*."[36] Commons thus implicitly poses a question, given growing scarcity of food and raw materials relative to rising world demand: Will Smith or Hobbes prevail?

In his conjectural model Hobbes so envisaged man's conception of felicity and his disposition to use power to achieve felicity as to make very evident the need for such restraints through civil law as only an *absolute* monarch could impose. Hobbes pointed to man's purported behavior in the state of nature where scarcity reigned. A man's "power" is defined as consisting in "his present means, to obtain some future apparent Good," these means comprising both his mental and his bodily faculties and such instruments as "Riches, Reputation, Friends, and . . . Good Luck." In the state of nature the individual's *right* to make use of this power to preserve "his own Nature" is unlimited; "there is nothing to which every man had not Right by Nature." Man tends therefore, so long as he is alive, to be animated by a "restless desire of Power after power"; for "felicity is a continuall progresse of the desire, from one object to another," and man "cannot assure the power and means to live well, which he hath present, without the acquisition of more." The resulting and continuing "Competition of Riches, Honour, Command, or other power, enclineth to Contention, Enmity, and War," so long as man remains in a state of nature and *unrestrained by the civil law of an absolute sovereign.*[37] In short, only a powerful apparatus of state can assure the order essential to a people's welfare, security, liberty, and conduct of economic affairs.[38]

Hobbes employed his conjectural model to represent that "Naturall Condition of Mankind" which obtains when there exists no "coercive Power" to abridge man's "naturall Liberty" and to curb his efforts to exercise dominion over others.

During the time men live without a common Power to keep them all in awe, they are in that condition which is called Warre; and such a warre, as if of every man, against every man.

In this state of war, which always assumes a potential when not an actual form, felicity and progress are well-nigh impossible of realization.

In such condition, there is no place for Industry; because the fruit thereof is uncertain: and consequently no Culture of the Earth, Navigation, nor use of the commodities that may be imported by Sea; no commodious

Building; no Instruments of moving, and removing such things as require much force; no Knowledge of the face of the Earth; no account of Time; no Arts; no Letters; no Society; and which is worst of all, continuall feare, and danger of violent death; and the life of man, solitary, poore, nasty, brutish, and short.

This condition of war arises from the fact that men, being generally equal in mental and physical ability and in their expectations respecting the attainability of sought ends and always remaining free to have recourse to Force and Fraud, seek each to satisfy fully his own wants and aspirations, even though the aggregate of their economic and other wants and aspirations far exceed what might be had even under conditions of peace.[39] Accordingly, even under conditions of peace, objects of man's desire would have to be rationed in some fashion that would insure balance between their supply and their utilization.

An absolutistic solution was derived by Hobbes from certain of Nature's purported laws. From natural laws requiring men "to seek Peace, and follow it," and "to defend" themselves "by all means," flowed the obligation each man was under to surrender his natural "right to all things; and be contented with so much liberty against other men, as he would allow other men against himself. Each man's right (or set of rights) was to be transferred to "a common power . . . with right and force sufficient to compell performance" on the part of all when a majority had covenanted to transfer to this power "such Rights, as being retained, hinder the peace of Mankind." This sovereign power—the Common-wealth—is the man, or an assembly of men that acts as one man or will, upon whom, through mutual covenant, the rights and strength of each have been conferred to the end that peace may be preserved. It is out of fear of compliance-enforcing action on the part of the sovereign that men accept abridgment of their liberty by civil law and "perform their Covenants made"; for in the absence of this fear, even though the keeping of covenants is an obligation under natural law, men would not keep them, compliance therewith running counter to their passions and their private interests which are at variance with the "common good."[40] In keeping with his analysis, justice, which is described by Hobbes as "a rule of Reason" and "a Law of Nature," is said to consist in "Keeping a Covenant," and injustice in "the not Performance of Covenant."[41] After all "Covenants, without the Sword, are but Words, and of no strength to secure a man at all." It was not, however, the function of justice, defined as compliance with liberty-restricting civil law, to remove all liberty and autonomy of individual action.

> For the use of Lawes, (which are but Rules authorised) is not to bind the people from all Voluntary actions; but to direct and keep them in such motion, as not to hurt themselves by their own impetuous desires, rashness, or indiscretion; as Hedges are set, not to stop Travellers, but to keep them in the way. And therefore a Law that is not Needfull, having not the true End of a Law, is not Good . . . . Unnecessary Lawes are not good Lawes; but trapps for Mony.[42]

Hobbes did not subscribe fully to the traditional definition of commutative justice as consisting in "proportion Arithmeticall" and "equality of value of the things contracted for," and of distributive justice as consisting in "proportion Geometricall" and hence "in the distribution of equall benefit, to men of equall merit."[43]

> As if it were Injustice to sell dearer than we buy; or to give more to a man than he merits. The value of all things contracted for, is measured by the Appetite of the Contractors: and therefore the just value, is that which they be contented to give.[44] And Merit (besides that which is by Covenant, where the performance on one part, meriteth the performance of the other part, and falls under Justice Commutative, not Distributive) is not due by Justice; but is rewarded of Grace only. And therefore this distinction, in the sense wherein it useth to be expounded, is not right. To speak properly, Commutative Justice, is the Justice of a Contractor; that is, a Performance of Covenant, in Buying, and Selling; Hiring, and Letting to Hire, Lending, and Borrowing; Exchanging, Bartering, and other acts of Contract.
>
> And Distributive Justice, the Justice of an Arbitrator; that is to say, the act of defining what is Just. Wherein, (being trusted by them that make him Arbitrator,) if he performe his Trust, he is said to distribute to every man his own: and this is indeed Just Distribution, and may be called (though improperly) Distributive Justice; but more properly Equity; which also is a Law of Nature.[45]

Equity consists, when something is divisible, in the "equall distribution to each man, of that which in reason belongeth to him"; when something is indivisible, in its enjoyment "in Common," by all if the quantity be sufficient, and "otherwise Proportionably to the number of them that have the Right"; and when something is neither divisible nor enjoyable in common, in distributing it by lot or according to some rule such as that of primogeniture or that of first occupancy.[46]

Hobbes does not define what constitutes distributive justice except to say that it consists in "Distributing to every man his own" and that it is realizable only under civil law and in a commonwealth of the sort Hobbes has described. Inequality too is described as having been "introduced by the Lawes civill," since men are equal by nature. Rights of "propriety" (i.e., property) being preservable only in a commonwealth, are not absolute against the sovereign. "Propriety," whether in land or commodities (among which "a man's Labour" is included), consisted in "a right to exclude all other subjects" from their use. The sovereign, however, could not be so excluded, since the right of propriety was had of the sovereign, and since exclusion of the sovereign would prevent his performing his office.[47] It was essential, in fact, Hobbes indicated, that the access of the commonwealth to the property of subjects not be quantitatively limited, since the requirements of the commonwealth could not be accurately enough foreseen. While he did not specify what constitutes an equitable distribution of income, he did indicate that the amount of taxes paid per person (whether by himself, or by another) should be equal inasmuch as his own defence was equally important to every man; and he did specify minimal charity for the disabled poor and enforced labor for the able unemployed.[48]

Hobbes' state could be made compatible in theory with a free-market economy as Hobbes implies. In reality, however, as Lord Acton and others have observed, power corrupts and absolute power corrupts absolutely. Whence we are left with the lack of an optimal distribution of functions between economy and polity and the power of keeping them so.

Hobbes' model did not win support for two reasons, substantive and a combination of the ideational and ideological. First, as Kuznets shows, the rate of growth of output increased markedly after the seventeenth century, especially in parts of Europe.[49] Of this Adam Smith (WN, pp. 70-74, 89, 189, 200-206, 322) as well as others were aware. Moreover, given the then system of communications and the disorganized state of the common man, aggregate aspirations and expectations tended no more than to keep pace with growth of aggregate income instead of growing faster as in today's world; nor was this outlook seriously changed by eighteenth-century optimism destined to be chilled by Malthus's more realistic outlook. Second, under the auspices of Locke and others, alternative political means to the security of the individual were put forward.[50] Locke's work was directed immediately against Sir Robert Filmer, the not very competent spokesman for absolutism fashionable among royalists who rejected Hobbes' view that government originated in contract and that the Church was a mere department of the state. Moreover, Locke viewed the state as a product of evolutionary growth, not as a response to anarchy; the state could serve as a source of collective conveniences, always with its powers limited by man's natural rights, particularly by his property rights. Finally, the prospects and hopes of the middle class, supporters of bourgeois opinion and values stressed by Locke, Cantillon, Quesnay, Hume, and others, brightened with improvement in their material conditions and prospects. Under the circumstances Hobbesian schemes had little to offer and much to take away from most of those who counted.

5. POSTLUDE

The two centuries that followed the appearance of Smith's work proved without historical parallel, witnessing a virtually unbelieveable growth of population and per capita income due both to man's learning how to exploit the world's abundance of natural resources available for development and to the growth and spread of the free enterprise system—a system that gave rein to the all-powerful force of self-interest within a socio-economic institutional context not very different from that which Smith would have considered optimal.[51] Indeed, were he to return, he would find confirmation of his counsel and anticipations in the first two centuries of our independence.

Today, however, finds these conditions changed. Well-founded fear of increasing biospheric scarcity has replaced confidence in the adequacy of the exploitable abundance of nature, a fear intensified by growth of world population and world demand for natural-resource-oriented products. Second, not only have modern economies become labor and trade-union dominated but the ideological, ideational, and institutional supports of the free-enterprise system have begun to crumble and the state has been usurping more and more of the responsibility for decisions and functions formerly centered in a relatively unshackled economy. Of these two changes, the second is by far the more important, since consciousness of scarcity and scarcity itself are in considerable part the product of state policies.

Emerging raw material scarcity, especially when intensified in its impact by cartellization and politicisation of international trade, tends to reduce international economic and political stability. Thus while high oil costs are proving especially burdensome in countries short of domestic food supplies and foreign exchange as well as disruptive of balance in international payments, the demand for foodgrain is outstripping its supply and is expected to exceed its supply by nearly one-fifth within fifteen years.[52] Meanwhile, growing pressure upon the biosphere and satisfaction of the often marginal wants of present generations at the expense of critical wants of future generations may be expected to produce intergenerational conflict.[53]

War, together with intellectuals, and democratic politicians dedicated to self-serving short-run considerations, has been contributing to the demise of a free society and its replacement by one which is already subordinating science and the flow of information to its control even as Sir Bernard Lovell has pointed out (*U.S. News & World Report*, Dec. 1, 1975, pp. 53-55). The post-1914 series of wars, as E. Halévy warned, has produced an era of tyranny inimical to free economies, destroyed the world political and cultural hegemony of Europe and Europe Overseas even as the Peloponnesian War destroyed Athenian hegemony, and has made increasingly probable nuclear war by the close of this century.[54]

In 1942 a perceptive Joseph A. Schumpeter called attention to the "crumbling walls" of capitalism, pointing in particular to the supposed "obsolescence of the entrepreneurial function," the destruction of both "protecting strata" and the "institutionalist framework of capitalist society," and to "growing hostility" of both intellectuals and "the social atmosphere of capitalism."[55] He referred also to "the vanishing of investment opportunity," an expected consequence of decline in the rate of growth of population and the demand for population-oriented investment. While population growth is likely to become negative and could present even problems associated with dissaving, it is to be noted that the state has absorbed an increasing fraction of GNP, about one-third in 1973 compared with about one-tenth in 1929, thus generating capital shortage. In 1973 about 47 per cent of federal outlay went for welfare and related purposes compared with 31 per cent in 1964 and an anticipated 55 per cent in 1981.[56] Moreover, increasing government spending tends to displace private spending.[57] Federal policies also contribute to municipal financial collapse (e.g., New York City).

As a result of ideological and ideational change the prevailing institutional structure no longer corresponds to one optimally compatible with an efficient free-enterprise economy. The state, formerly essentially an order-maintaining institution, has metastasized into a Robin Hood-like apparatus largely concerned with the usurpation and redistribution of funds in response to those who have temporarily captured control of the apparatus of state or are hopefully waiting in the wings for their turn. Meanwhile, the population has fallen into a variety of self-serving groups—trade unions, business and professional associations, ideological collectivities, all quarreling

over the contents of the fleshpots instead of concerning themselves with keeping the pots filled, truly a Hobbesian world.
Furthermore, there has been a heavy transfer of decision
making from the market with its effective feedback and
penalty-reward system to the state and its agencies which are
virtually immune to penalties for poor performance and hence
have little incentive to perform well.[58] The state apparatus has
become overloaded with financially uncompensated demands
as well as with decision making it is unsuited to undertake.[59]
Moreover, this task is complicated by increasing egalitarianism[60]
and the emergence of a market outside Smith's major concern,
namely, that within which common-property situations are
produced by non-exclusive rights.[61]

The dominant elements of the private economy appear to
be developing in ways Lenin had in mind when he indicated
that continuing inflation would destroy the bourgeois economy
and that the capitalist in search of profit might fall within the
foils of collectivists. Lenin did not, of course, anticipate that
the welfare-cum-laborist state, together with luxury, might
eventually destroy initially among children and eventually
among private and public employees the very discipline and
responsibility essential to the survival of a free enterprise
economy and society. Illustrative of the course of affairs is
the fact that a "trade union has definitely decided to distribute
sign-up cards to 700,000 Army, Navy and Air Force reservists"
(*Durham Morning Herald,* Jan. 14, 1976, p. 4A). Associated
with and interacting with dissipative welfare-oriented and
laboristic trends is ever more emphasis by policy formulators
and the polity upon the Present and Near-Future to the neglect
of the Future and disregard of lessons of the Past (e.g.,
destruction of social security and retirement systems by premature retirement and steady increase in the beneficiary/
contributor ratio).

Growing disequilibrium between economy and polity—
against which Smith warned—tends to be reenforced by changes
within the structure of the private enterprise system itself.
Organizational complicatedness appears to be weakening the

feedback system animating the dinosaurian corporation,[62] a system essential to the economic health of such an organization. Moreover, what could be a "new American ideology" may be weakening corporate decision-making power.[63] Furthermore, spread of economic control by the very large, technocratically dominated corporation may be crowding out many small entrepreneurs who not only possess entrepreneurial skill, imagination, flexibility, but also manifest a healthy animus toward our strangling state bureaucracy and ever expanding government borrowing and spending and the resulting "crowding out" of private borrowing and investment.

Associated with these trends and growing disequilibrium between economy and polity is the emergence of a system of income distribution based not so much upon productive performance as upon political clout and the power to interrupt almost at will the essential continuity of the flow of economic activity. The resulting struggle for increase in income shares, when combined with politics-ridden monetary and fiscal policies, generates continuing inflation which in turn destroys critical business information and intensifies conflict between buyer and seller and between employer and employee.[64] In time, of course, under these conditions a Hobbesian solution takes on an ever more attractive albeit misleading mien than a subverted Smithian ideal.

It is easy, however, especially in an ahistorical age such as our own, to be misled. So a prescient Aesop warned his contemporaries more than two thousand years ago. Aesop relates how Jupiter appointed a log as nightwatchman king of the frogs. King Log, however, was content to float around and not bother his subjects. In time, however, each frog wanted more of the National Product than he was turning out. So various frogs organized themselves into groups and sought some of their neighbors' portions, especially the portions of their less organized and more helpless neighbors. Some of the latter in turn organized. A state of continuing war, together with destruction of productive power and private property, came into being. Finally the frogs, blind to the fact that they had produced strife instead of ample goods and services, asked Jupiter to replace King Log with a powerful, absolutist ruler. So Jupiter appointed a stork king of the frogs. Whereupon King Stork deprived the frogs of their liberty and property and ate them whenever he was of a mind to do so.

NOTES

1. J.C. McManus, "The Costs of Alternative Economic Organizations," *Canadian Journal of Economics 8* (August 1975): pp. 334-50.

2. J.J. Spengler, "Laissez Faire and Intervention: A Potential Source of Historical Error," *Journal of Political Economy 57* (1949): 438-41.

3. Cited by H.E. Jacob in *Six Thousand Years of Bread* (New York: Doubleday, Doran and Co., Inc., 1945), p. 1. Cf. Peter Laslett, *The World We Have Lost* (London: Methuen and Co. Ltd., 1965), p. 126.

4. George Sabine, *A History of Political Theory* (New York: Henry Holt and Co., Inc., 1937), chapter 10, esp. p. 179. See also R.D. Cumming, *Human Nature and History* (Chicago: University of Chicago Press, 1969), chapters 1, 5, and 7.

5. See Hannah Arendt, *The Origins of Totalitarianism* (New York: Harcourt, Brace and Co., 1951).

6. E.g., see B.A. Saletore, *Ancient Indian Political Thought and Institutions* (London: Asia Publishing House, 1963), esp. Part 3.

7. E.g., see Fung Yu-Lan, *A History of Chinese Philosophy*, trans. Derk Bodde (Princeton: Princeton University Press, 1952), 1, chapter 13, and *The Book of Lord Shang*, trans. J.J.L. Duyendak (Chicago: University of Chicago Press, 1963).

8. *The History of Herodotus*, trans. George Rawlinson (London: J.M. Dent and Sons, Ltd., 1936), Book 1, chapter 97.

9. *The Complete Writings of Thucydides* (Modern Library, New York, 1934), Book 1, chapter 1, pp. 3-4.

10. Carl Menger, *Problems of Economics and Sociology*, trans. F.J. Nock, edited with Introduction by Louis Schneider (Urbana: University of Illinois Press, 1963), esp. Book 3 and Appendix 8. John Austin's concern was the definition of sovereign and sovereignty—than which there is no other—and not that of Hobbes. E.g., see Sabine, *History*, pp. 654-55; T.E. Holland, *Jurisprudence*, 12th ed. (New York: Oxford University Press, 1917), p. 50.

11. See J.M. Buchanan, "What Should Economists Do?" *Southern Economic Journal 30* (January 1964): 213-22; J.R. Commons, *Institutional Economics* (New York: The Macmillan Company, 1934); Peter M. Blau, *Exchange and Power in Social Life* (New York: J. Wiley, 1964).

12. Joseph J. Spengler, "Herodotus on the Subject Matter of Economics," *The Scientific Monthly 81* (December 1955): 276-77; Marcell Mauss, *The Gift* (Glencoe: The Free Press, 1954), pp. 20-21, 45, 69.

13. E.g., see F.H. Heichelheim, *The Ancient Economy* (Leiden: A.W. Siuthoff's Vitgeversmij, N.V., 1957); M.A. Copeland, "Concerning the Origin of a Money Economy," *The American Journal of Economics and Sociology 33* (January 1974): 1-18; W.H. Leemans, *The Old-Babylonian Merchant* (Leiden: E.J. Brill, 1950), chapter 2; K.R. Veenhof, *Aspects of Old Assyrian Trade and Its Terminology* (Leiden: E.J. Brill, 1972).

14. M.I. Finley, *The Ancient Economy* (Berkeley: University of California Press, 1973), pp. 28-29, also pp. 22-23.

15. C.L. Cochrane, *Christianity and Classical Cultural* (New York: Oxford University Press, 1944), pp. 43-50, chapter 4; Cicero, *De Officiis* (Cambridge, Mass: Harvard University Press, 1947) Book 1, p. 7; Book 3, p. 12; H. Michell, "The Edict of Diocletian: A Study of Price Fixation in the Roman Empire," *Canadian Journal of Economics and Political Science 13* (February 1947): 1-12.

16. Cochrane, *Christianity*, p. 316.

17. See R.W. Southern, *The Making of the Middle Ages* (London: Hutchinson's University Library, 1953), pp. 41-49, 76; R.S. Lopez and I.W. Raymond, eds., *Medieval Trade in the Mediterranean World* (New York: Columbia University Press, 1961); S.D. Goiten, *A Mediterranean Society* (Berkeley: University of California Press, 1967); M.M. Postan, E.E. Rich and E. Miller, eds., *The Cambridge Economic History of Europe*, vol. 3 (Cambridge: Cambridge University Press, 1967).

18. In the prologue to his code Hammurabi describes its purpose to be "to cause justice to prevail in the land, to prevent the strong from oppressing the weak . . . to further the welfare of the people," while in the code itself specific regulations were set down. See R.F. Harper, *The Code of Hammurabi, King of Babylon* (Chicago: University of Chicago Press, 1904), p. 3.

19. E.A. Havelock, *The Liberal Temper in Greek Politics* (London: Jonathan Cape, 1957), chapters 11-13; Cicero, *De Officiis*, Book 3, csp. ibid., p. 6, on interests men have in common.

20. See Barry Gordon, *Economic Analysis Before Adam Smith* (New York: Barnes and Noble, 1975), chapters 1-3; Joseph Soudek, "Aristotle's Theory of Exchange. An Inquiry into the Origin of Economic Analysis," *Proceedings of the American Philosophical Society 96*, no. 1, (February 1952): 64-68.

21. *Institutes of Justinian*, 1: pp. i, 1, and 3, trans. J.B. Moyle, 5th ed. (Oxford, 1937); S.T. Worland, *Scholasticism and Welfare Economics* (South Bend: University of Notre Dame Press, 1967), chapter 8-9 and *passim;* Cochrane, *Christianity*, pp. 39, 48ff., 76ff., 103, 150, 191-96.

22. Gordon, *Economic Analysis*, chapters 5-9; Worland, *Scholasticism*, chapters 8-9. See also under "price." *The Theodosian Code*, trans. with commentary by Clyde Pharr (Princeton, 1952).

23. Rudolph Sohm, *The Institutes*, trans. J.C. Leslie, (Oxford: Clarendon Press, 1907), pp. 22, 24.

24. E.g., see Jacob Viner's essay in J.M. Clark et al., *Adam Smith 1776-1926* (Chicago: University of Chicago Press, 1928), pp. 116-55; C.R. Fay, *The World of Adam Smith* (Cambridge: W. Heffer and Sons, Ltd., 1960), Eli Ginzberg, *The House of Adam Smith* (New York:

Columbia University Press, 1934); also Joseph J. Spengler, "The Role of the State in Shaping Things Economic" in *The Tasks of Economic History,* supplement, *Journal of Economic History* 7 (1947) : 123-43.

25. William Letwin, *The Origins of Scientific Economics* (London Methuen and Co., 1963), chapter 8, p. 221.

26. Ibid., p. 228.

27. H.A. Simon, *Models of Man* (New York: John Wiley and Sons, 1957), chapters 14-15.

28. Joseph J. Spengler, "The Problem of Order in Economic Affairs," *Southern Economic Journal* 15 (July 1948): 1-29.

29. A.N. Whitehead, *Science and the Modern World* (New York: The Macmillan Company, 1925), pp. 74-75. This fallacy consists in "mistaking the abstract for the concrete."

30. Basil Willey, *The Seventeenth Century Background* (New York: Garden City, 1953), pp. 188-89.

31. Whitehead, *Science,* chapter 3.

32. Ibid., p. 5.

33. See J.J. Spengler, "The Role of the State," *loc. cit.*

34. Cf. Sohm, *Institutes,* pp. 22-25.

35. E.g., see Commons, *Institutional Economics,* pp. 4-8, 37-40, 108-24, 128-58.

36. Ibid., p. 141.

37. *Leviathan* (1651), (New York: Everyman's Library), pp. 24-25, 30, 43, 49-50, 66-70.

38. Ibid., chapters 20-21, 24, 29.

39. Ibid., chapters 13, 17 and pp. 35, 50, 74, 79-80, 87, 96; also chapter 24 on the economy of a commonwealth. Although population growth operated to augment this discrepancy, it could be offset for a time by colonization. "And when all the world is overcharged with Inhabitants, then the last remedy of all is Warre; which provideth for every man, by Victory, or Death." Ibid., p. 185.

40. Ibid., chapter 17 and pp. 66-67, 70-74, 92, 141-42.

41. Ibid., pp. 74, 76, 87.

42. Ibid., p. 185.

43. Ibid., pp. 77-78.

44. Ibid., p. 78. Elsewhere "the value . . . of a man . . . his price . . . so much as would be given for the use of his Power [is] a thing dependent on the need and judgment of another. . . . And as in other things, so in men, not the seller, but the buyer determines the Price." Ibid., p. 44. No restraint upon the buyer or the seller is indicated at this point. Elsewhere (ibid., p. 177) "monopolies" are bracketed with tax-farmers and implicitly charged with sometimes over-charging for their services to the detriment of the commonwealth; and (p. 122) export-import monopolies are described as buying domestic products monopsonistically and as selling imports monopolistically whereas the welfare of the commonwealth required that there be "liberty at home, every man to buy, and sell at what price he could" and that monopsony and monopoly be practiced only in traffic carried on abroad.

45. Ibid., p. 78.

46. Ibid., pp. 80-81.

47. Ibid., pp. 74, 79-80, 93-94, 130-31, 173, 183-84.

48. Ibid., pp. 183-89.

49. Kuznets, Simon, *Economic Growth of Nations: Total Output and Production Structure* (Cambridge, Mass.: Harvard University Press, 1971), chapter 1.

50. E.g., see John Locke, *Of Civil Government* (1960), (New York: Everyman's Library, 1936), and W.G. Carpenter's Introduction; also Talcott Parsons' illuminating account in his *Structure of Social Action* (New York: McGraw-Hill Book Co., 1937), chapter 3.

51. On the growth of income and population since 1776 see Simon Kuznets, *Economic Growth of Nations* (Cambridge: Harvard University Press, Belknap Press, 1971).

52. E.g., see Lester R. Brown, "The World Food Prospect," *Science 190* (December 12, 1975): 1053-59; C. Fred Bergsten, "The New Era in World Commodity Markets," *Challenge* (September-October 1974): 34-42; S.J. Burki and S. Yusuf, "Population: Exploring the Fertility Link," *Finance & Development 12* (December 1975): 29-32; A.D. Crockett and D.M. Ripley, "Sharing the Oil Deficit," ibid.: 12-16.

53. See Nicholas Georgescu-Roegen, "Energy and Economic Myths," *Southern Economic Journal 61* (January 1975): 341-81.

54. See "Nuclear War by 1999?" *Harvard Magazine* (November 1975): 19-25, a discussion by five experts; E. Halévy, *The Era of Tyrannies* (Garden City, N.Y.: Doubleday and Co., Inc., 1965), pp. 265-85, written in 1936, and pp. 209-48 on World War I.

55. *Capitalism, Socialism, and Democracy* (New York: Harper and Bros., 1942). For critiques see C.O. Hardy, "Schumpeter on Capitalism, Socialism and Democracy," *Journal of Political Economy 53* (December 1945): 348-56; and *An Appraisal of the Fatalistic View of Capitalism*, issued in 1944 by the Machinery and Allied Products Institute. See also E. C. Ladd, Jr., and S.M. Lipset, *The Divided Academy* (New York: McGraw-Hill Book Co., 1975); Daniel Bell, *The Cultural Contradictions of Capitalism* (New York: Basic Books, 1976).

56. D.J. Ott et al., *Public Claims on U.S. Output* (AEI Institute) (Washington, D.C., 1973), p. 12; *The Annual Report of the Council of Economic Advisers, 1974* (Washington, D.C., 1974), pp. 324-25.

57. K.M. Carlson and R.W. Spencer, "Crowding Out and Its Critics," *Review* of Federal Reserve Bank of St. Louis *57* (December 1975): 2-17.

58. See J.J. Spengler, "Economist vs. Legist, Politician, Bureaucrat," *Atlantic Economic Journal 2* (November 1974): 1-14.

59. M.J. Crozier et al., *The Crisis of Democracy* (New York: New York University Press, 1975), chapters 2 and 5.

60. A.M. Okun, *Equality and Efficiency: The Big Tradeoff* (Washington, D.C.: Brookings Institution, 1975). A much stronger case against egalitarianism may of course be made.

61. J.H. Dales, "Beyond the Market Place," *The Canadian Journal of Economics* 7 (November 1925) : 483-503.

62. Christopher Stone, *Where the Law Ends: The Social Control of Corporate Behavior* (New York: Harper and Row, 1975).

63. George C. Lodge, *The New American Ideology* (New York: Alfred A. Knopf, Inc., 1975).

64. J.J. Spengler, "Inflation, Regulated Industry, and the American Economy," *Proceedings* of the Thirteenth Annual Iowa State Regulatory Conference on Public Utility Valuation and the Rate Making Process, May 21-23, 1974, Ames, Iowa, pp. 80-95.

The Justice of Natural Liberty

James M. Buchanan
VIRGINIA POLYTECHNIC INSTITUTE
AND STATE UNIVERSITY

1. INTRODUCTION

THE 1976 bicentennial of the publication of Adam Smith's *The Wealth of Nations* occurs amid a still-accelerating discussion of the principles of justice, stimulated in large part by John Rawls. His catalytic book, *A Theory of Justice,* published in 1971,[1] has caused economists, along with other social scientists and philosophers, to devote more attention to "justice" in the first half-decade of the 1970s than in perhaps all of the preceding decades of this century combined. This discussion has been hailed as the return of political and social philosophy to its former status of intellectual interest and respectability. My purpose in this paper is to re-examine Adam Smith's norms for social order, notably for justice, and especially as these may be related to the modern post-Rawlsian discussion. I want, in particular, to evaluate Smith's "system of natural liberty" in terms of criteria for justice that are akin to those employed by Rawls.

I am indebted to my colleagues, Victor Goldberg, Nicolaus Tideman, Gordon Tullock and Richard Wagner for helpful comments on earlier drafts of this paper. A version of this paper was published in *Journal of Legal Studies* V (January 1976), 1-16.

In order to do this, it will first be necessary to define, as fully as is possible, Smith's underlying model or paradigm for social interaction, a paradigm that was influenced by the historical setting of Scotland in the 1770s. In addition, it will be useful to discuss briefly Smith's methodology. Once these steps are taken, we can outline Smith's ordering of the priorities for reform. From this we should then be able to suggest how a returned Adam Smith might view our society in 1976, and how his modern ordering of reform priorities might differ from those two centuries removed. This imagined Smithian stance may then be compared and/or contrasted with that of John Rawls. In what may be surprising, and especially to those who are only casually familiar with the works of each man, I shall demonstrate that the similarities outweigh the differences. A returned Adam Smith would be a long distance from the modern libertarian anarchists, and even from the espousal of the minimal state described by Robert Nozick.[2] But John Rawls is also a long distance from the position which has been attributed to him, that of being a "defender of the liberal welfare state, somewhat modified in the direction of greater egalitarianism."[3] These philosophers would surely be closer to each other than either would be to the image which intellectual fashion has imposed upon him.

2. THE REAL AND CONCEPTUAL WORLD OF ADAM SMITH

Adam Smith was one of the leading figures of the Scottish Enlightenment, which suggests that his interests were in no way provincial. His intent in *The Wealth of Nations* was to offer a readily-generalizable criticism of what he labeled the "policy of Europe." But he lived and worked, nonetheless, in eighteenth-century Scotland. Because his writings, and again notably *The Wealth of Nations,* retain so many elements of direct and current relevance, it is easy for the modern reader to neglect the necessary influences of time and place on his analysis as well as on his normative priorities.

What were the essential structural characteristics of the society that Adam Smith observed? Almost two centuries would elapse before a popular tract could condemn an "affluent society." The industrial revolution, with its technological counterpart, was in its very early and formative stages. Indeed its full achievements might never have become reality save for the impact of some of Smith's own ideas. The modern corporation was foreshadowed only in the government-sponsored international trading companies. Still largely agricultural, Britain was only becoming "a nation of shopkeepers."

The society that Smith observed was highly stable relative to that of our own century. This society was also very poor by twentieth-century standards; Smith's analysis was applied directly to what we would now call a "developing" or an "underdeveloped" society. The expansion in material goods generated by the technological revolution of the post-Enlightenment era was not predictable in 1776. Most men were born to live, work, and to die in the same local community.

Some appreciation of this historical setting is helpful in any attempt to define Smith's working model for social interaction. Two central elements of this model or paradigm may be isolated here, elements which are important in understanding his conceptions of justice. The first of these involves what we should now call the utility of income to the individual. Smith did not use this terminology and he was not intellectually hidebound by the now-dominant orthodoxy which largely neglects basic questions about the meaning of utility itself and then proceeds to impose a particular form on the utility function. Instead, Smith carefully distinguished between that which drives men to action, the promised or anticipated utility from an increasing stream of real goods and services, or from a growing stock of assets, and that which measures the actual satisfactions secured subsequent to the receipt of such incremental flows and stocks. Beyond a certain level of real income (a level which was, nonetheless, presumably out of reach for the average or representative member of the working class), the anticipated marginal utility of income to an individual exceeds the realized marginal utility. This divergence constituted, for Smith, the great deception which was essential in driving the whole system, which acted to insure that self-interest would, in fact, generate increasing prosperity and economic growth.[4]

In some sense, therefore, differentials in measured or received incomes among individuals and among social classes or groups were, to Adam Smith, considerably less important than to his counterpart who inhabits the modern welfare state. Smith was not nearly so ready to translate these into differences in achieved satisfaction, happiness, or well-being. And who is to attribute the naiveté to Adam Smith in this respect? The balance is not on one side alone.

Smith expressed little or no normative concern with income differences among persons; he was primarily concerned with the absolute levels of income generated, and with the differences in these levels among time periods, that is, with growth. He did infer a direct relationship between the aggregate income generated for the whole society and the well-being of the laboring classes.

There is a second element of Adam Smith's model for social interaction that is helpful in evaluating his conceptions of justice. Smith did not assume or postulate significant differentials in capacities among human beings. The differences between the "philosopher and the street porter" were explained largely in terms of upbringing, training, and education. In the current debates, Smith would find himself arrayed squarely on the side of those who stress environmental factors and who play down the relevance of genetic endowments. Smith was also writing before Cairns and Mill had developed the economic theory of noncompeting groups. In his conceptual model, individual income differences (at least as regards wage or salary incomes) were explained largely in "equalizing" terms. That is to say, in an operative "system of natural liberty" the observed differences would be those that would be predicted to emerge when all persons freely exercised their choices among occupations and employments. By implication, at least for the members of the laboring class, in such a system all persons would be equally advantaged at the onset of making career and occupational choices.

3. THE SCOTTISH METHOD

A.L. Macfie makes the distinction between what he calls the Scottish method, characteristic of Adam Smith's approach to problems of social policy, and the scientific or analytical method which is more familiar to modern social scientists.[5] In the former, the center of attention lay in the society as observed, rather than in the idealized version of that society in abstraction. As I have suggested above, Adam Smith did have an underlying model or paradigm for social interaction; he could scarcely have discussed reforms without one. But his interest was in making the existing social structure "work better," in terms of the norms that he laid down, rather than to evaluate the possible limitations of the structure as it might work ideally if organized on specific principles. Frank Knight suggested that critics of the enterprise system are seldom clear as to whether they object to market order because it does not work in accordance with its idealized principles or because it does, in fact, work in some approximation to these principles. Applied to Adam Smith, his position was straightforward. He was critical of the existing economic order of his time because it did not work in accordance with the principles of natural liberty. He was not, and need not have been, overly concerned with some ultimate evaluation of an idealized structure.

Smith's methodology has been turned on its head by many modern scientists. The post-Pigovian theory of welfare economics has largely, if not entirely, consisted in a search for conceptual flaws in the workings of an idealized competitive economic order, conceived independently of the flawed and imperfect order that may be observed to exist. Partial correctives are offered in both the theory of the second-best and in the still-emerging theory of public choice, but the perfect-competition paradigm continues to dominate applied economic policy discussions.

This methodological distinction is important in our examination of Smith's conception of justice. In one sense, John Rawls' efforts in defining and delineating "a theory of justice" are akin to those of the neoclassical economists who first described the idealized competitive economy. (I am not, of course, suggesting that Rawls' attempt has had or will have comparable success or even that the basic subject matter is amenable to comparable analytical treatment.) By contrast, Adam Smith saw no need of defining in great detail the idealized operation of a market system, and of evaluating this system in terms of strict efficiency criteria. Similarly, he would have seen no need of elaborating in detail a complete "theory of justice," of defining those principles which must be operative in a society that would be adjudged to be "just." In comparing Smith with Rawls, therefore, we must somehow bridge the contrasting methodologies. We can proceed in either one of two ways. We can make an attempt to infer from Smith's applied discussion of real problems what his idealized principles of justice might have embodied. Or we can infer from John Rawls' treatment of idealized principles what his particular applications of these might be in an institutional context. In what follows, I shall follow both these routes.

4. JUSTICE AS SECURITY

Adam Smith did not publish the book on jurisprudence that he had projected, although a student's notes from his lectures apparently include most of the material that might have been incorporated.[6] In these lectures, "justice" was listed as only one of the four great objects of law. In the section specifically on justice, Smith referred almost exclusively to the relatively narrow conception of security. "The end of justice is to secure from injury."[7] In this context, the treatment seems quite different from that of John Rawls, for whom "justice is the first virtue of social institutions."[8] But the difference can be exaggerated, even here. Smith explicitly calls attention to security as a necessary attribute of any well-functioning society, and he reflects common-sense usage of the term "justice" in his discussion. Rawls, two centuries later, takes this aspect of justice more or less for granted, and shifts his discussion to another level. He would, presumably, agree fully with Smith that any just society would also require security of person and property. Rawls' primary interest is "beyond justice" in the more restricted definition employed by Adam Smith.[9]

Their difference lies in the fact that Smith did not make a comparable extension. Distributive justice, in the modern meaning of this term, is largely neglected by Smith, at least in terms of explicit treatment. This is explained, in part, by Smith's underlying presuppositions about utility differences, noted above, and, in part, by the relatively greater importance appropriately assigned to economic development in the eighteenth-century setting. As I shall demonstrate, however, Smith's suggestions for policy reforms generate distributive results that may be reconciled readily with Rawlsian criteria. We need not accept Jacob Viner's interpretation that writers in the Scottish tradition were minimally interested in reform, in the modern meaning of this term.[10]

5. NATURAL LIBERTY

Adam Smith explicitly rejected a contractarian explanation for the emergence of government and for the obligation of persons to abide by law, preferring, instead, to ground both on the principles of authority and utility.[11] Furthermore, he did not recognize the possible value in using conceptualized contract as a benchmark or criterion with which to evaluate alternative political structures. However, his device of the "impartial spectator" serves this function and it is in many respects akin to the conceptualized contract. Smith's norms for social order were not strictly utilitarian, in the Benthamite sense, and justice was an important attribute, justice which embodied the security to person and property previously noted but extending beyond this when his whole structure is considered.[12] Beyond security, Adam Smith would have surely ranked "natural liberty" as his first principle of justice.

To hurt in any degree the interest of any one order of citizens for no other purpose but to promote that of some other, is evidently contrary to that justice and equality of treatment which the sovereign owes to all different orders of his subjects.[13]

In several applied cases, he makes clear that violations of natural liberty are unjust.[14]

Before doing this, however, it may be helpful to digress somewhat. Smith's great work, *The Wealth of Nations,* has been widely interpreted as being informed normatively by efficiency criteria. This emphasis is broadly correct, provided that the efficiency norm is not given exclusive place. Smith's purpose was to demonstrate how the removal of restrictions on free market forces and the operation of his "system of natural liberty" would greatly increase the total product of the economy and, more importantly, how this would generate rapid economic growth, thereby improving the lot of the laboring classes. What is often missing from this standard interpretation is Smith's corollary argument, sometimes implicit, to the effect that this system of natural liberty would also promote his ideal of justice. Failure to allow individuals to employ "their stock and industry in the way that they judge most advantageous to themselves, is a *manifest violation of the most sacred rights of mankind.*"[15] There was, to Smith, no trade-off between "efficiency" and "equity," in the more familiar modern sense. As a general principle of social order, the freedom of individual choice would produce efficiency; but it would also be a central attribute of any social order that was just.

My emphasis in this paper is on this aspect of Smith's argument because I want to compare his first principle of "natural liberty" with Rawls' first principle of "equal liberty." Smith's method forces us to look at his examples rather than to expect to find any elaborated discussion of the concept per se. These suggest that Adam Smith was by no means an eighteenth-century Robert Nozick, who conceived natural moral boundaries to individuals' rights and who claimed that any invasion of these rights was unjust. The Smithean system of natural liberty is not anarchy, either the Hobbesian war of each against all or the more confined Rothbard-Nozick setting where individuals mutually respect the boundaries of each other. "Boundary crossings," to employ Nozick's helpful terminology here, violate Smith's natural liberty in some cases but such violations must be assessed in essentially pragmatic terms. Smith's sanctioned violations of natural liberty did not seem invariant to the environmental setting in which individuals might find themselves.

Almost by necessity, we look at Smith's treatment from the vantage point of modern welfare economics. When we do so, his limits to the exercise of natural liberty seem to coincide surprisingly with those extensions of potentially warranted collective action that might be laid down by a careful and sophisticated application of externality analysis. To Smith, there is clearly an unwarranted invasion of natural liberty if an individual's (any individual's) freedom of choice is restricted when there are no demonstrable spillover damages on others in the community. On the other hand, Smith sanctioned interferences with individual freedom of choices when the exercise of such choices (for example, the building of walls that were not fireproof) "might endanger the security of the whole society."[16] Smith explicitly stated that such latter restrictions on individual choices may be "considered as in some respect a violation of natural liberty," but that such choices ought to be "restrained by the laws of all governments."[17]

Adam Smith distinguished between what we would now call pecuniary and technological externalities. His approved interferences with natural liberty extended only to those cases where genuine technological externality could be demonstrated, and he quite explicitly stated that possible pecuniary spillovers gave no cause for restrictions on trade.[18] It would, of course, be absurd to suggest here that Smith's final array of potentially justifiable interferences with the freedom of individual choices corresponds fully with that which might be produced by the modern welfare economist. Furthermore, his own array of examples of potentially warranted interferences with natural liberty would surely be different in 1976 from that of 1776.

On balance, however, there seems no question but that Smith's implied analysis of potential restrictions on the freedom of individual market choices can be made reasonably consistent with modern efficiency analysis, utilizing Pareto criteria for meaningful improvement. That is to say, even if Pareto optimality or efficiency is held up as the only relevant norm, many of Smith's particular examples would qualify. What is important for my purposes, however, is that Smith sanctioned interferences only when efficiency criteria overweighed those of justice, conceived here not in distributional terms at all, but in terms of the value of natural liberty. If we leave aside considerations of administration and enforcement, modern economic analysis would suggest the introduction of restrictions when overall efficiency is enhanced, with no explicit recognition of the necessary trade-off with individual freedom of choice. With Adam Smith, by contrast, any restriction on the freedom of individuals "may be said [to be] a manifest violation of that natural liberty, which it is the proper business of law, not to infringe, but support."[19] Possible efficiency gains must, therefore, be reckoned against the costs in liberty, in "justice" in the broader sense here considered.

In evaluating his own work, there is some evidence that Adam Smith considered *The Wealth of Nations* to be a demonstration that the "system of natural liberty," which emerged more fundamentally from normative criteria of justice, could *also* meet efficiency criteria.[20] It is perhaps our relative overconcentration on his major treatise that causes modern interpreters to overlook the noneconomic, or more generally, the nonutilitarian, foundations for the "natural system of perfect liberty and justice."[21]

6. RAWLS' PRINCIPLE OF EQUAL LIBERTY

Smith's principle may be compared with John Rawls' first principle of justice, that of "equal liberty," to which he assigns lexicographical priority over his second principle. These two principles or conceptions of liberty are, in practice, substantially equivalent although, strictly speaking, and perhaps surprisingly, Rawls must be classified as a more ardent *laissez faire* theorist than Smith. This is due to Rawls' lexical ordering of the principle of equal liberty as prior to his distributive precept. Smith, by comparison, inserts a threshold before marginal trade-offs can be considered, a threshold beyond which invasions of apparent natural liberty might presumably be sanctioned. But their positions are similar in that neither Smith nor Rawls is utilitarian in the sense that final evaluation is reduced to a single standard. To Smith, the "impartial spectator" would not condone piecemeal interferences with natural liberty even if aggregate social production is thereby maximized. To Rawls, the maximization of expected utility is rejected as the objective, even behind a genuine veil of ignorance.

The principle of equal liberty, as presented by Rawls, is stated as follows:

Each person is to have an equal right to the most extensive total system of equal basic liberties compatible with a similar system of liberty for all.[22]

In his discussion Rawls emphasizes the implications of this principle for political institutions (e.g., for equality of franchise, for freedom of speech and press), but he tends to neglect the comparable implications for economic institutions, which were, of course, central to Adam Smith's concern. In several places, Rawls does state that the principle of equal liberty suggests a market system, but he does not go on to particular examples or cases.[23] Nonetheless, any attempt to apply the Rawlsian principle must lead to a condemnation of many overt restrictions on individual choices that have been and may be observed in the real world. Particular interferences that would, in this way, be classified as "unjust" by Rawlsian criteria would correspond very closely to those which Smith classified in the same way. Consider only two of the most flagrant modern-day examples. The uniform minimum wage regulations imposed by the Congress under the Fair Labor Standards Act, as amended, would clearly be "unjust" under either Rawlsian or Smithean criteria. Mutually-agreeable contractual terms between unemployed persons (notably teenagers) and potential employers are prohibited, with an absence of comparable restrictions on others in society.[24] Or, consider the regulations of the Interstate Commerce Commission in restricting entry into trucking, clearly an invasion of the natural liberty of those who might want freely to enter this business as well as a violation of the principle of equal liberty. The listing could be readily extended to such institutions as tenure in universities, restrictive licensing of business and professions, prohibition or sumptuary taxation of imports, subsidization of exports, union shop restrictions in labor contracts, and many others.

It is unfortunate that Rawls did not see fit to discuss more fully the application of his first principle to such institutions, especially since his treatise and general argument have attracted such widespread attention from social scientists generally. Economists have continued to call attention to the inefficiency of these institutions, but, since Smith, they have rarely called attention to their fundamental injustice.[25] Had they, or Rawls, done so, these institutions might have proved more vulnerable to criticism than they have appeared to be.

Difficulties arise when we attempt to apply the Rawlsian principle of equal liberty to those restrictions on individual choices that might be plausibly defended on familiar externality grounds. As noted above, Smith's less constraining norm allows natural liberty to be violated under some circumstances, provided that the costs are properly reckoned. But Rawls' lexical ordering prevents this sort of trade-off, even with the insertion of an appropriate threshold. Consider, for a real-world example, the closing of the Saltville, Virginia plant of the Olin Corporation in the early 1970s as a result of governmentally-imposed water-quality standards. Local residents were left unemployed; long-term contractual agreements between these persons and Olin were terminated, clearly a restriction on liberties. Presumably, defense of this governmental action was based on the alleged benefits of improved water quality to the general population of the whole country. It does not seem possible to stretch Rawls' principle of equal liberty to cover such instances. The liberties of some persons were restricted for the alleged benefits of others, and without appropriate compensation. There was no trade-off with other liberties, as Rawls might have required; the defense could only have been advanced on utilitarian-efficiency grounds. To Rawls, this governmental action could only be classified as "unjust."[26]

Working from the principle of equal liberty alone, therefore, and keeping in mind the lexical priority assigned to this in his whole construction, we must conclude that John Rawls is far from the "defender of the liberal welfare state" that he has been made out to be, and, indeed, that his implied institutional structure for the economy closely resembles that which was first described by Adam Smith. Only a "system of natural liberty," a regime of effectively operating free markets, could meet Rawlsian requirements for "equal liberty," and, through these, for "justice."

7. DISTRIBUTION AND JUSTICE

Rawls has been misinterpreted in this respect because of his relative neglect in elaborating the implications of his first principle for economic institutions and, more importantly, because of his relative concentration on the second principle that he adduces, that which addresses the distribution of the social product. It is here that Adam Smith and John Rawls seem most apart, and Rawls explicitly discusses the system of natural liberty only to reject it in favor of what he terms the system of democratic equality.[27] But we need to see precisely wherein these two philosophers diverge. I shall try to demonstrate that, once their methodological differences are acknowledged and once their empirical presuppositions are fully exposed, there need be little variance in their assessments of reform priorities in a 1976 setting.

We can perhaps best commence by examining the distributional consequences of Adam Smith's system of natural liberty, under the empirical presuppositions that Smith himself adopted. In 1776, a very large part of the total population was made up of members of the laboring classes, and Smith did not think that inherent differences in capacities were significant. The economic position of an average or representative member of this group could best be improved by allowing markets freely to emerge and to operate, by removing all, or substantially all, restrictions on trade, and by eliminating all constraints on the flow of resources, human and nonhuman, among alternative uses. Such a system would predictably

generate differences in incomes among separate members of
the laboring classes, but these would tend to equalize the
relative advantages of separate employments. Those who were
not members of these classes, those employers who accumulate
capital and utilize it productively in hiring labor, would secure
differentially higher incomes from profits. But Smith makes
it clear that it is precisely the attraction of such incomes which
drives the whole process, which insures that the economy grows
and prospers. Even here, however, Smith raises some questions
about the efficacy of exceptionally high incomes from profits,
and he warns against the tendency toward profligacy that such
excesses create.[28] Smith is not clear on the possible allo-
cative role played by rental incomes secured by landowners.
Given his pre- but quasi-Ricardian model of the economy,
he probably would not have been opposed to taxes on
land rent.

There are distributional consequences of Smith's system,
but, strictly speaking, the *distribution* of product among social
classes or among members of any one class is clearly secondary
to *production,* to securing maximal national income. This was
to be accomplished by the removal of disincentives throughout
the economy. The overriding objective was to increase the
economic well-being of the member of the laboring classes,
while adhering to the precept of justice which the system of
natural liberty represented.

At first glance, Smith's system seems a world apart from
the Rawlsian setting, where the emphasis is on distribution,
with production being largely neglected. The difference
principle of distribution, appended lexically to that of equal
liberty, states that inequalities in access to primary goods are
acceptable in the just society only in so far as they are shown to
be advantageous to the least-advantaged members of the
community. But, in the empirical setting postulated for Adam
Smith, what would an application of this Rawlsian difference
principle have implied? An argument for a tax on land value
might have been produced, along with an argument for taxation
of excessively high incomes from profits, with a redistribution
of proceeds generally to members of the laboring classes.

Perhaps more importantly, from his discussion of the favorable effects of less restrictive laws of land ownership and transfer in the English as opposed to the Spanish and Portugese colonies, we may infer that Smith would have supported legal reforms designed to open up prospects for greater mobility of persons between the land-owning and nonowning groups.[29] Such reform implications of his system could have been readily accepted by Smith, who might, however, have treated such reforms as being of piddling importance relative to the more fundamental steps which involved the removal of governmental constraints on individual liberty.

Rawls projects the distributional issue to center stage perhaps because he presumes, empirically, that there exists only a relatively remote relationship between the pattern of income receipts, and of asset holdings, in society and the aggregate size of the total product. Furthermore, he seems to assume that there exists a distribution of natural or inherent capacitie. among persons, a distribution which tends to generate non-equalizing income-wealth differentials that carry with them neither economic nor moral justification. In the Rawlsian paradigm, the philosopher is not merely an educated porter.

The "system of natural liberty" which Rawls explicitly discusses, and rejects, is not that of Adam Smith.[30] Rawls uses this designation to refer to a system which embodies economic efficiency (Pareto optimality) as its only objective, and his critical remarks suggest that he does not impose the constraints that are made quite explicit in Smith. Rawls does not examine Smith's system in itself, but from his more general discussion we may infer that his central objection would be focused on the dependence of distributional outcomes on initial asset holdings, or initial endowments. Before treating this point in some detail, I re-emphasize that Rawls does not criticize the market-determined distribution of product, given the set of initial endowments, a source of much confusion in the continuing critique of social institutions.[31] His attention is concentrated, properly, on the pre-market distribution of endowments to which, contrary to Nozick, Rawls attributes no moral qualities.

Adam Smith did not discuss the distribution of initial endowments, but for his system of natural liberty to meet the Rawlsian precepts for justice in the postulated Rawlsian setting, two conditions would have to be met. First, any deliberately imposed change in the basic institutions of society designed to bring about greater equality in initial endowments must be shown to worsen the position of the least advantaged. It does not seem likely that this condition could be fulfilled.[32] Even here, however, it should be recognized that the most glaring inequalities in initial endowments could scarcely arise in a genuine system of natural liberty. How many great family fortunes would exist had not the government employed its power to enforce and to police monopoly privileges? Secondly, there would have to be a direct relationship between the economic position of the least-advantaged members of society and the total income generated in the economy. This condition seems more likely to be met, regardless of how the "least-advantaged" members are to be defined, provided only that the difference principle is applied in a dynamic setting.[33] Institutional changes that tend to retard or to stifle economic growth seem likely to harm the position of the least-advantaged rather than to improve it, almost regardless of the motivation for such changes.[34]

I do not want to make Adam Smith and John Rawls seem to be more similar in their basic philosophical positions than a careful interpretation of their published works might warrant. Even when we take into account the historical and methodological distance between them, and even when we try to apply their criteria for justice in the converse empirical settings, we cannot legitimately infer a Smithean distributional interest comparable to Rawls. In 1976, a returned Adam Smith might or might not be an egalitarian of Rawlsian stripe. Because of his relative underemphasis on the relationship between material goods and human happiness, the most judicious evaluation suggests that Smith would not have been motivated to stress distributional inequities to the extent of Rawls. It also seems clear that, even in the affluence of 1976, Smith would have paid considerably more attention to the net benefits measured in terms of both efficiency and justice, to be secured by a dismantling of restrictions on freedom of individual choices.

Finally I should note a possible difference in the implications of a commonly-shared philosophical rather than empirical presupposition for normative discourse. Even if he should have recognized, empirically, that persons differ, and substantially so, in basic capacities, Adam Smith might well have argued that such inequalities have no place—and in fact must be presumed away—in the process of designing a just and viable social order. The basic institutions of society must be based on the presumption that men are "equals" in some fundamental generic sense.[35] This is the attitude that clearly informs the United States Declaration of Independence, and the coincidence of dates between this and the publication of *The Wealth of Nations* is not merely historical accident. From this presumption or presupposition, undue concern with distributional outcomes might be considered to be, at base, aberrant. In this light, the onus would be on John Rawls to defend his concentration on the distributional principle as appended to the principle of equal liberty rather than on Adam Smith to defend his failure to make a comparable extension.

8. CONCLUSIONS

I have had several objectives in this paper. First of all, I have tried to show that Adam Smith's system of natural liberty, interpreted as his idealized paradigm for social order, embodies justice as well as economic efficiency. Indeed Smith may well have conceived his masterpiece to be an argument to the effect that the system which was acknowledged to embody justice could also be efficient. Secondly, I have attempted to compare Smith's first principle of natural liberty with John Rawls' first principle of equal liberty. Although I have not tried to examine an exhaustive list of examples here, a straightforward application of either of these principles implies significant restrictions on the propriety of governmental-political interference with the freedom of individuals to make their own economic decisions. My ultimate, and perhaps most important purpose has been to use the timely discussion of Adam Smith's precepts for justice as a vehicle for correcting what has seemed to me a grossly neglected aspect of John Rawls' much-acclaimed and much-discussed book. Both Smith and Rawls are libertarians in that principles of liberty hold positions of priority in their orderings of objectives. Neither is utilitarian in the Benthamite or even in the more constrained Paretian sense of this term. The differences between Smith and Rawls lie in the fact that Smith's discourse is concentrated on the efficiency-producing results of natural liberty; the corollary attributes of justice are not stressed. And, for the several reasons noted, the distributional results are not explicitly evaluated against criteria of justice. On the other hand, Rawls treats liberty sketchily despite the lexical priority assigned to it, and he concentrates on the distributional qualities of an idealized social order. Translated into practical reform proposals, however, both philosophers accept an effectively-operative market economy as a basic institution in any society that could be classified as just.

The differences in distributional emphasis are important, but I have shown that these are at least partially explained by differences in empirical and possibly philosophical presuppositions. One implication of the comparison should be that a libertarian position is not inconsistent with an egalitarian one, despite attempts to make these seem contradictory by both the libertarian-antiegalitarians and the collectivist-egalitarians. A strong defense of the liberties of individuals, which can only be secured in an operating market economy, may be joined with an equally strong advocacy for the reform of basic social institutions designed to produce greater equality among individuals in their initial endowments and capacities. This is how I interpret John Rawls' position, which comes close to that associated with Henry Simons,[36] whose explicit emphasis on free markets is clearly akin to that of Adam Smith. If my interpretation is accepted, the normative distance between Adam Smith and John Rawls is surely less than the sometimes careless comparisons of images would suggest.

NOTES

1. John Rawls, *A Theory of Justice* (Cambridge: Harvard University Press, 1971).

2. Robert Nozick, *Anarchy, State and Utopia* (New York: Basic Books, 1974).

3. Marc F. Plattner, "The New Political Theory," *The Public Interest* 40 (Summer 1975): 120.

4. For the most direct statement on this, see Adam Smith, *The Theory of Moral Sentiments,* with an Introduction by E.G. West (New Rochelle: Arlington House, 1969), pp. 263-65.

5. A.L. Macfie, *The Individual in Society: Papers on Adam Smith* (London: Allen and Unwin, 1967), p. 19.

6. Adam Smith, *Lectures on Justice, Police, Revenue and Arms.* Edited by Edwin Cannan (Oxford: Clarendon Press, 1896).

7. Ibid., p. 5.

8. John Rawls, *Theory of Justice*, p. 3.

9. Cf. Rawls, ibid., p. 7.

10. See Jacob Viner, "Guide to John Rae's *Life of Adam Smith,"* published with John Rae, *Life of Adam Smith,* Reprints of Economic Classics (New York: Augustus M. Kelley, 1965), p. 112.

11. Adam Smith, *Lectures on Justice*, pp. 11-13.

12. For a good discussion on this, see A.L. Macfie, *Individual in Society,* pp. 68-71.

13. Adam Smith, *The Wealth of Nations* (Modern Library edition), p. 618. All subsequent references are to this edition. Note the similarity of this statement of Smith to John Rawls' definition of the principle of equal liberty, cited below.

14. See *The Wealth of Nations,* pp. 121-22 (on apprenticeship requirements); p. 141 (on restrictions on migration); p. 497 (on entry restrictions), as examples.

15. *The Wealth of Nations,* p. 549. (Italics supplied.)

16. *The Wealth of Nations,* p. 308.

17. Ibid.

18. See, in particular, his discussion on page 342 of *The Wealth of Nations,* where he rejects imposing restrictions on entry into retailing trades even "though they [shopkeepers] may so as to hurt one another."

19. *The Wealth of Nations,* p. 308.

20. In Rae's citations from the notes of John Millar, one of Smith's best students, there is the following passage:

> In the last of his lectures he examined those political regulations which are founded, not upon the principle of *justice* but that of *expediency,* and which are calculated to increase the riches, power, and prosperity of a state. Under this view he considered the political institutions relating to commerce, to finances, to ecclesiastical and military establishments. What he delivered on these subjects contained the substance of the work he afterwards published under the title of *An Inquiry Into the Nature and Causes of the Wealth of Nations.*

See John Rae, *Life of Adam Smith* (New York: Augustus M. Kelley, 1965), p. 55.

21. *The Wealth of Nations*, p. 572.

22. Rawls, *Theory of Justice*, p. 250.

23. "I assume in all interpretations that the first principle of equal liberty is satisfied and that the economy is roughly a free market system." Rawls, *Theory of Justice*, p. 66.

24. Minimum wage legislation would also be unjust by Rawls' second principle since the primary groups harmed are those who are least-advantaged, those with relatively low economic productivity.

25. In his treatise on liberty, F.A. Hayek does not represent liberty or freedom as an attribute of "justice," but rather as an independent "source and condition of most moral values." (p. 6) At one point (p. 99), however, he does suggest that justice requires something akin to the Rawlsian principle of equal liberty. Cf. F.A. Hayek, *The Constitution of Liberty* (Chicago: University of Chicago Press, 1960).

26. I do not suggest that the idealized Rawlsian constitution could not allow for escapes from the genuine externality-public goods dilemmas that fully independent private adjustments might produce. Such a constitution would require that such escapes be accomplished through more inclusive contractual agreements, which would, of course, embody compensations to those who might be harmed by change. My point in the text here is to indicate that the Rawlsian principle of equal liberty would not allow for governmentally-imposed changes without compensation, regardless of the benefit-cost ratios.

27. Rawls, *Theory of Justice*, pp. 65-75.

28. This aspect of Smith's argument is stressed by Rosenberg. See Nathan Rosenberg, "Some Institutional Aspects of *The Wealth of Nations*," *Journal of Political Economy 68* (December 1960): 557-70.

29. See *The Wealth of Nations*, pp. 538-39.

30. Rawls, *Theory of Justice*, pp. 65-75.

31. For my own explicit discussion of this point, see my paper, "Political Equality and Private Property: The Distributional Paradox," prepared for conference on Markets and Morals, Battelle Memorial Institute, Seattle, May 1974. Published in *Markets and Morals*. Edited by G. Berwent, P. Brown and G. Dworkin (New York: Hemisphere Publishing, 1977), pp. 69-84.

32. An argument to this effect could be plausibly advanced with respect to certain of the more obvious proposals. One such argument that might possibly be extended in this way relates to the confiscatory taxation of inheritances. See Gordon Tullock, "Inheritance Justified," *Journal of Law and Economics 14* (October 1971): 465-74.

33. Critics of Rawls have pointed to the ambiguities that arise in defining "least-advantaged," and Rawls has acknowledged the difficulties involved when dynamic or intergenerational issues are introduced. Even if the "least-advantaged" are defined to be those members of society who are wholly nonproductive, growth-retarding policies will violate the difference principle if the intergenerational discount rate is sufficiently low.

The indigent of the 1970s are in a better position than they would have been had a Rawlsian difference principle of justice been applied, without consideration of the intergenerational impact, in the 1870s.

34. The "quality of life" or environmental regulations that have now become widespread seem to offer the best examples. These institutional changes are acknowledged to have differentially harmed those who are in differentially disadvantaged economic positions. Quite apart from possible violations of the principles of equal liberty, these changes would have to be classified as unjust by the difference principle.

35. For a discussion of this presumption of fundamental equality, even in the context of empirical inequalities, see my *The Limits of Liberty* (Chicago: University of Chicago Press, 1975), especially pages 11-12.

Rawls, of course, accepts this presumption in his basic contractarian derivation of the principles of justice. The presumption is not at issue here. The possible difference lies in the implications of this presumption for distributional norms.

Care must be taken to distinguish a presumption of equality in some "original position" and/or in some basic philosophical sense, and the elevation of distributional equality as an ideal attribute of the just society. Rawls is somewhat vulnerable on this count, especially because he derives his principles of justice from "fairness" notions. In so far as "fairness" applies to the rules of games, by extension to ordinary games, it becomes questionable to speak of achieved or final equality as an ideal. This would amount to "condemning a footrace as unfair because someone has come out ahead." On this point, see Frank H. Knight, *The Ethics of Competition* (London: Allen and Unwin, 1935), p. 61.

36. See Henry Simons, *Economic Policy for a Free Society* (Chicago: University of Chicago Press, 1948) and *Personal Income Taxation* (Chicago: University of Chicago Press, 1938).

There are some ambiguities in Rawls which make my interpretation less persuasive than might appear. He does not seem to recognize the necessary relationship between an operative market economy and the dispersion of property ownership. For this reason, particular sections of his treatise may be interpreted as collectivist in flavor. (See, especially, Rawls, *Theory of Justice*, pp. 271-72.) On balance, these seem to me to represent failures to follow through carefully the full implications of the first principle of equal liberty.

Justice, Liberty and Economy

Leonard Billet

UNIVERSITY OF CALIFORNIA, LOS ANGELES

THE *Wealth of Nations* is fundamentally concerned with the question, what is a just economy? References to justice and injustice, equity and oppression appear so frequently in Adam Smith's treatise that it is surprising to note the absence of the just economy theme in scholarly commentary on *The Wealth of Nations.*[1] Yet the persistent moral and political elements in his political economy are neither paradoxical nor ornamental. Adam Smith considered his treatise to be a work of political science and an instrument of political reform. He had intended to write a comprehensive work on jurisprudence or "the theory of the general principles which ought to run through and be the foundation of, the laws of all nations," which, he said, was "of all sciences by far the most important."[2] Smith referred to *The Wealth of Nations* as a partial fulfillment of his grand design.

In order to comprehend the basic moral and political framework of Adam Smith's economic thought, one must refer to his first book, *The Theory of Moral Sentiments,* published in 1759. It is in this work that Smith most explicitly argues the unique importance of justice for understanding the nature of society and government. "Justice," he asserts, "is the main pillar that upholds the whole edifice. If it is removed, the great, the immense fabric of human society...must in a moment crumble into atoms."

Society may subsist, though not in the most comfortable state, without beneficence: but the prevalence of injustice must utterly destroy it.[3]

Since the rules of justice are the foundation of social order, the central theme of political inquiry, including political economy, must be the nature of justice.

According to *The Theory of Moral Sentiments,* the moral nature of man and his intrinsic sense of justice make society possible, necessary and desirable: possible because all community must be based on some shared standards of right and wrong which can be enforced, necessary because man cannot be his social and moral self apart from society, and desirable because only in society can the potentialities of his nature be more fully developed. The "natural sense of justice," ultimately founded on the "general fellow feeling which we have with every other man, merely because he is our fellow creature,"[4] instills in mankind a rejection and resentment against unmerited injuries whether done to oneself or to others. Smith's conception of justice, like Plato's, presupposes that certain things are *due* to people. His notion of justice, however, is much more narrowly defined than Plato's. Both thinkers perceive justice as inhering in the polity, for Plato because political and moral community are the same, and for Smith, because they are not. Justice, in Smith's view, is essentially concerned only with that part of what is morally due mankind which ought to be enforced by governing authority; it is therefore the virtue "of which the observance is not left to the freedom of our wills, [and] which may be [legitimately] extorted by force."[5] For Smith, the basic question raised by justice is: which rules and institutions are most appropriate to human society, and in particular, to the economic order of production and consumption?

Smith's political economy is predicated on the theory of the nature and significance of justice presented in his work on morality. *An Inquiry into the Nature and Causes of the Wealth of Nations* is an attempt to express "the rules which the natural sense of justice would dictate" for the economic order, so that they might be embodied in positive law. Adam Smith referred to his own system of principles and institutions as the "liberal plan of equality, liberty and justice,"[6] "the natural system of perfect liberty and justice,"[7] and the system of "natural liberty and justice."[8]

More than ever, Smith's "liberal plan" needs to be re-examined from the perspective of its moral and political foundations. The following considerations on the moral justifications for economic liberty and their relationship to labor and capital, the role of government within the system of natural liberty and the powerful anti-colonialism of *The Wealth of Nations* are intended to be a contribution to this undertaking.

JUST LIBERTY

Everyone knows that Adam Smith is the apostle of economic liberty. However, few seem to recognize that, for Smith, liberty, competition, and the market process are derived from and subordinate to principles of social justice. Justice necessarily circumscribes liberty, and the unrecognized central theme of *The Wealth of Nations* is *just* liberty. Smith believed that just liberty is a necessary condition for the most creative and efficient production. Underlying this belief is the prior question: why is liberty morally necessary in the economic order? To answer this question, one must begin with his view of man and society, for like all justice theorists, he analyzes and evaluates social rules and institutions in relation to their appropriateness to human nature.

For Smith, human nature is complex, multi-dimensional, inherently conflictive and incapable of perfection. Innate social or "fellow-feeling" capacities necessarily lead mankind to be concerned with the situation and views of others. From this bond the *possibility* of justice is derived. On the other hand, powerful anti-social elements and capacities such as "envy, malice and resentment," "hatred, anger, [and] spite . . . drive men from one another." Though man is a "rational creature" and reason is "capable of counteracting the strongest impulses of self-love,"[9] reason is hard to sustain and mankind is prone to be blinded by passions and the "misrepresentations of self-love." Above all, humans are active, creative, imaginative and choosing beings, i.e., 'self' expressive individuals. Each person has his own inner "principle of motion."[10] From these complexities, the *necessity* for justice is derived.

Smith believed that "man's natural love for society," moral socialization and the enforcement of just laws could contain and inhibit the expression of anti-social tendencies while permitting the social, prudent and humane virtues to develop. But if governing authorities presumed the governed to be like pieces on a chess board—rightfully moved by the will and force of others—people could never fully be 'themselves' or realize their potentials. Self-expression and self-determination in the economic order, as well as in political and religious life, are considered to be essential constituent principles of just social institutions.

Smith's view that the imaginative, choosing and self-expressive nature of man requires just economic liberty also helps to explain the oft-overlooked moral basis of self-interest in *The Wealth of Nations*. This principle of action is a necessary foundation for a just economy precisely because he sees that self-interest is intrinsically connected with choice, reason and self-determination. To the extent that the individual is free to own and use his labor and capital resources, to that extent he will be free to be guided by his own conceptions and desires regarding purpose and benefit. As Smith views it, the choice lies between self-determined and "other-determined" interest as a moral foundation for economic activity. Furthermore, self-interest, the active form of proper self-love, is not a vice. Proper self-love or prudence, "the care of health, of the fortune, of the rank and reputation of the individual," is sharply distinguished from avarice or greed. In addition, economic self-interest coexists with the benevolent other-regarding passions which are also intrinsic expressions of the human personality.

Economic self-interest is assumed to operate within a context of moral rules, religious beliefs and the restraints of civil law and justice which have as one important purpose, among others, preventing human beings from injuring each other. These powerful forces are not suspended in *The Wealth of Nations,* although the focus on economic order and self-interested activity has misled many into ignoring them. These forces inhibit immorality and injustice by directly affecting the character of the inner man through education, socialization and indoctrination or by the threat of punishment, religious as well as civil. It is within this context that "every man, as long as he does not violate the laws of justice, is left perfectly free to pursue his own interest his own way, and to bring both his industry and capital into competition with those of any other man, or order of men."[11]

Economic institutions, unlike these other more important social structures, cannot *prevent* evil. But certain kinds of economic order can channel the operation of self-interest in such a way that its consequences are beneficial to society as well as to the individual. This is the purpose of economic liberty and the competitive market. Smith thought that the great defect of feudal, mercantilist and other economic arrangements was that they created, encouraged or supported opportunities for a few to aggrandize themselves at the expense of the "great body of the people." His reliance on self-interest "expresses his faith in the value of the individual and in the importance of freeing the individual man from the fetters of outworn economic institutions.[12]

According to Smith, the pursuit of self-interest or prudential behavior is itself an already socialized process, (i.e., based on taking others into consideration) as J.R. Lindgren has demonstrated. Those involved in economic activity tend to subordinate the impulse of their self-loving passions in accordance with public opinion, and to conform to the expectations of others through a desire for praise. "They regard the pursuit of riches not as the most efficient way to maximize their own satisfactions, but simply as the right way to behave."[13] Even within the context of prudential activity directed towards the pursuit of wealth, self-interest is not exclusively self-orientation in regard to the *results* of such efforts. Self-interest is perfectly consistent with, indeed is often the inspiration for, persons using their goods or resources for the benefit of others through support of the arts and sciences, education, political movements, religious activities or institutions, etc.

The Wealth of Nations also justifies the competitive free market economy as a long-range solution to the important problem of correcting and reforming maldistributions of wealth arising from past injustices. Smith thought of the system of natural liberty as a method of "rectification of injustice in holdings," to use the philosopher Robert Nozick's term. Nozick has argued in a recent work that a comprehensive theory of justice must have, as one of its elements, a principle for rectifying past injustices involving the acquisition and transfer of property.[14] Smith believed that the operation of a market economy accompanied by the abolition of legal privilege, monopolies, corporations, laws fixing wages and inhibiting mobility would tend gradually to reform and redistribute both land and other forms of wealth in the direction of a more equitable and widespread system of ownership.

In Western Europe, the ownership of landed property was, in large part, the unjust heritage of conquest and usurpation, according to Smith. Laws such as entail and primogeniture hindered economic processes from "reforming" or breaking up and dispersing these originally unjust concentrations of property and power. "They prevent the division of great estates, and thereby hinder the multiplication of small proprietors [and] keep so much land out of the market, that there are always more capitals to buy than there is land to sell, so that what is sold always sells at a monopoly price."[15] Such regulations were "founded upon the most absurd of all suppositions, the supposition that every successive generation of men have not an equal right to the earth and all that it possesses."[16] Abolishing restrictions on land ownership and its marketability would extend the possibilities of proprietorship to greater numbers of people who could purchase land with wealth more justly accumulated. While all the evils of the past could not be immediately rectified, the ownership of land

and other forms of wealth could eventually be broadened considerably and put on new and more just foundations. With the extension of small proprietorship, which Smith considered the most desirable type of property system, the great estates and aristocratic families might wither away, a process which undoubtedly would be hastened by habits and a way of life more conducive to spending than producing wealth. Through the market process, land could be "transferred" to people of more modest means who were able and desirous of using it productively.

Perhaps even more important, Smith believed that wealth derived from commercial and manufacturing activities was also, in significant part, the product of social injustices. Class legislation, legal privileges and monopoly rights in trade and production distorted the "natural proportion. . . between judicious industry and profit." He looked to competition and the market principle to halt the growth of unjustly accumulated wealth, to undermine politically determined sources of economic advantage and to prevent the entrenchment of established industry which, he thought, always has a tendency to seek official "protection," i.e., legal means of preservation from the possibility of competitive displacement. Since most wealth founded on legal privileges could not long be expected to withstand free competition, the system of natural liberty would tend to operate to transform and to weaken the power of the past over the present and future.

The Wealth of Nations' negative evaluation of the joint-stock company or corporation is best understood in this perspective. To Smith, the corporate form, a special and unique creation of positive law, was inherently fraught with serious dangers. Corporations were very attractive to investors because they promised a "total exemption from trouble and risk beyond a certain sum," were able to "draw to themselves much greater stock than any private copartnery," and could undertake activities beyond the capabilities of small numbers of individuals.[17] But this very limitation of liability and 'artificial' concentration of resources gave the corporation an unfair advantage over non-corporate and smaller owner-operated enterprises, which are the necessary mainstay of a competitive free market economy. Though it might be advantageous or profitable to the individuals involved, Smith did not think the corporation was generally a socially advantageous institution. It created and perpetuated a class of proprietors or investors "who seldom pretend to understand anything of the business of the company; and when the spirit of faction, happens not to prevail among them, give themselves no trouble about it, but receive contentedly such half-yearly dividends, as the directors think proper to make them."[18]

Smith did not believe the law should encourage "ownership divorced from management" or benefit without responsibility. Both monopoly and the corporate form tended to erode the multiplication of ownerships, the diffusion of independence and interdependence of enterprise, the dispersal and diversification of capital and labor and of opportunities for creativity and access to productive activity which he considered to be essential aspects of a just economy. From the point of view of a more egalitarian, creative and efficient, freely competitive and responsible economy, Adam Smith saw no moral basis for the corporation and the unrestrained development of corporate privilege.

LABOR AND CAPITAL

When Marx commented in his early writings that Engels was correct in calling Adam Smith the "Luther of political economy," he was referring to Engels' recognition that *The Wealth of Nations* represented a radically new political economy "which recognized labour as its principle" and which understood that "labour is the sole essence of wealth."[19] The very opening sentence of Smith's treatise asserts the fundamental role of labor in the productive life of every community.

The annual labour of every nation is the fund which originally supplies it with all the necessaries and conveniencies of life which it annually consumes, and which consists always either in the immediate produce of that labour, or in what is purchased with that produce from other nations.[20]

Although Adam Smith was not the first to notice the importance of labor, he decisively liberated economic thought from certain sterile notions about the nature and causes of wealth by placing labor and its productive powers in the center of the creative process. "It was not by gold or silver, but by labour, that all the wealth of the world was originally purchased."[21]

Smith considered labor to be not only the source and cause of wealth, and the "real measure" of exchangeable value, but ultimately the "real wealth of the society."[22] Though aware of the dark side of the division of labor, especially the threat of moral and intellectual stultification which accompanied its growth, he nevertheless considered it to be indispensible to raising the living standards of the vast majority of the people.

For Adam Smith, the activity of labor, the division of labor and the productivity of labor are not only 'technical' conditions of economic life and progress, they are the moral bases of economic activity and institutions. Labor or "strength and dexterity," "toil and ingenuity" is an essential aspect of human self-expression and societal development. Therefore, that system of political economy is most just which allows the greatest scope for persons to labor in accordance with their capacities and aims, and which, as much as possible, enables them to gain the reward or "produce" of their labor.

The human capacities of strength and skill, imagination, toil and ingenuity are the ultimate foundation for all just ownership of property, according to Smith. "The property which every man has in his own labour, as it is the original foundation of all other property, so it is the most sacred and inviolable."[23] Natural differences in the ability and/or willingness to labor, an existential reality, is the fundamental source of inequality of property. Thus, labor is the natural and just basis for inequality of property. Inequality, however, tempts some to commit acts of injustice against property, no matter how legitimately it has been acquired through toil and effort. It is therefore necessary that the "valuable property which is acquired by the labour of many years, or perhaps of many successive generations" be protected from the "injustice" of others "by the powerful arm of the civil magistrate."[24]

Just ownership of property is ultimately a consequence of human self-possession and self-expression. Smith views property, where it is morally defensible, to be based on the ideas of justice, self and labor. Freedom includes the possibility of acquiring property and Smith held to the view (of Montesquieu) that where men are able to own property, they are not likely to be the property of others. And if, unlike Marx, he does not consider labor as *the* expression of man's humanity, it is nevertheless a kind of human expression which is of decisive practical and moral significance in economic life.

Given Smith's emphasis on the significance and value of labor, the concern over the position and condition of the laboring classes which pervades his treatise should not occasion great surprise. It is true that Smith viewed labor as "the principal claimant, among the several producing groups in society to the sympathies of both the social scientist and the public administrator."[25] What is puzzling to some is his acceptance and justification of capital and profit. Was it not Smith himself who stated:

> In that original state of things, which precedes both the appropriation of land and the accumulation of stock, the whole produce of labor belongs to the labourer. He has neither landlord nor master to share with him.[26]

Yet, in "commercial society" the labourer cannot enjoy the whole produce of his own labour but "must in most cases share it with the owners of the stock who employs him." According to Heilbroner, this acceptance of capital and profit clearly indicates Smith's ideological narrowness and the "essentially 'class-bound' nature of his social vision."[27]

Perhaps so, but when Smith abandons the "original state of things" in which the laborer enjoyed the whole produce of his labor, apparently without much regret, it is because he believed that the "fall" into capital, wages and profit is 1) a natural (uncoerced) result of the previous social condition, and 2) a necessary condition for increasing the living standard of the laborer. First, according to Smith, capital and profit are legitimate consequences of the human ability to reason and calculate. Under social conditions where people are able to own and control their own labor and its products and are desirous of and free to improve the material conditions of life, capital and profit tend to develop. The idea and process of "exchange," which brings motivation, calculation and reason into creative relationship with one another, provides a proximate moral basis for capital and profit. While much notice has been taken of the "propensity to truck, barter, and exchange one thing for another" as the "principle which gives occasion to the division of labor," the role of exchange as a significant basis for Smith's moral economy of liberty and justice is less widely appreciated. Though exchange may not appear to be a moral notion, in fact its normative connotations are critical both to Smith's and Marx's political economy.

For Marx, the very idea and activity of a calculated exchange of goods and services involves a distortion of man's true nature. In his view, the only acceptable "labor" is that which involves an expression of man's being for the purpose of directly fulfilling his "needs." Exchange is essentially sordid. It is by the standard of a future exchangeless, though still productive world, that Marx condemns the economic ideas and arrangements of his time and most of previous history. But if for Marx exchange violates "being," for Smith it can express an important aspect of man's creative nature and may therefore serve as a legitimate foundation for economic order and progress. And while for Marx exchange is a form of slavery, according to Smith the natural human ability to exchange one's labor and its products actually has become the instrument for gradually freeing mankind from arbitrary dependence upon others for their subsistence, i.e., from slavery and feudal institutions. In past ages, he argued, the livelihood of the vast majority of people depended on the will and power of wealthy individuals or institutions. Whereas "in the present state of Europe," though a rich and powerful person contributes to the support of very many people, "they are all more or less independent of him . . . because generally they can all be maintained without him."[28]

In an exchange society, every person through the possession of his own labor is naturally provided with something valuable and productive that *he* controls and can use for his own benefit in the light of his own determinations. The universal possession of the ability to labor dictated universal freedom to employ one's labor. Labor and exchange tended to undermine arbitrary and unjust inequalities of wealth. Labor and liberty would bring "comfort and conveniences" to the masses. With higher living standards, and widespread education, a greater equality of opportunity for individuals and societies to freely develop would result. For Adam Smith, the larger meaning of the principle of exchange (and the division of labor) was that it had the potential to deliver man from subordinated dependence to a more egalitarian interdependence. He believed that this was the economic direction in which European society had been moving since the Middle Ages.

The fact that opportunities to use one's own resources are inevitably structured and ordered by society underlay Smith's attack on the political economy of his day for unjustly restraining these opportunities for many, especially the laboring classes. Man's desire for more control over his own life, for greater and more equal opportunity and for freedom from servility and arbitrary dependence on others for his livelihood, remained unfulfilled. Smith urged the adoption of the principles of natural liberty in order to greatly enlarge the scope and strengthen the progress towards independence and interdependence.

When the principles of liberty and self-determined interest are combined with those of labor, exchange, and legitimate inequality of property, capital and profit are likely to result, according to Smith. Though inequality of property does not necessarily lead to capital, it is a basis for capital or that part of a person's or society's wealth employed to produce additional goods. If this process of capital accumulation or reproduction is prohibited or hindered, then the living standards of an individual or a society must remain at the same or nearly the same level.

Capital is not necessary "in that rude state of society in which there is no division of labour, in which exchanges are seldom made, and in which every man provides everything for himself."[29] Labor is central to production, prior to capital and to ownership of property and is itself the source of property, inequality and capital. All economies produce goods though they do not necessarily produce capital. Every economy must have workers but need not have capitalists.

But *The Wealth of Nations* emphatically stresses the importance of capital and capital accumulation to the development of the productive processes of society. The desire to *increase* the production of goods and services, the desire for "development" in other words, and the aim of enhancing the productive powers of labor and the social abilities of man to cooperate and exchange, which is the core of that process, inevitably brings capital into the very center of economic life. The division of labor, Smith emphasized again and again, was the immediate source of improvement and wealth. To it was owed the "invention of all those machines by which labour is so much facilitated and abridged." Every established division of labor and every step forward in specialization, cooperation, and improving the tools of production requires an accumulation of capital, according to Smith. Increased capital investment per worker is the basis for increased output per worker. Furthermore, capital accumulation and investment increase the demand for labor and therefore the wages of labor. Higher wages provide an incentive for owners to improve the productivity of labor resulting in lower prices for consumer goods, thus indirectly augmenting the purchasing power of the working class.

Smith's fundamental concern respecting productivity was the relationship between a "given" amount of labor or industry and its output. The purpose of capital was to "facilitate and abridge," not to increase the intensity of labor or the length of the working day, as Marx supposed. The justification for capital was that either a "smaller quantity of labour produce[s] a greater quantity of work," or that the "same quantity of industry produces a much greater quantity of work."[30] Capital contributed to the benefit of individuals and to the social good by putting greater numbers to work at higher wages and by encouraging more efficient organization and "automation."

Only the advantageous employment of capital made it possible for a nation to "maintain the greatest quantity of productive labour, and increase the most, the annual produce of the land and labour of that country."[31]

In essence, the laborer is better off when he does *not* get the whole produce of his labor. "In a savage nation every one enjoys the whole fruit of his own labour, yet their indigence is greater than anywhere."[32]

Compared, indeed with the more extravagant luxery of the great, his accomodation must no doubt appear extremely simple and easy; yet it may be true, perhaps, that the accomodation of an European prince does not always so much exceed that of an industrious and frugal peasant, as the accomodation of the latter exceeds that of many an African king, the absolute master of the lives and liberties of ten thousand naked savages.[33]

Because of the increased productivity of labor, based on the institutions of exchange, capital, and profit, the laborer has traded his own little mud pie for a slice of a larger and more nourishing cake.

THE ROLE OF GOVERNMENT

It is true that *The Wealth of Nations* is primarily concerned with removing obstacles to economic liberty and competition and not with the problem of legislation directed towards the protection and operation of a system not yet completely established. Since these obstacles were in large part legal and political, prompted by special interests and founded on an inadequate understanding of economic relationships, Smith was preoccupied with exposing injustices and explaining the nature of competitive market principles.

Free, however, from the belief in the perfection of man's nature, Smith could not but be free from the idea of the perfection of the market economy and its supposed ability to provide *all* the "goods" required by a good society or even all those services necessary to sustain the system of natural economic liberty itself. A philosopher who thought that due to the "prejudices of the public" and "what is more unconquerable, the private interests of many individuals," to expect the complete establishment of his system was "as absurd as to expect that an Oceana or Utopia should ever be established,"[34] may be accused of undue pessimism, but he is unlikely to assume that those same forces of prejudice and interest would disappear with the growth of economic liberty. Further, if we remember that, according to Smith, the established interests, "the merchants and manufacturers" in particular, are always and everywhere engaged in a "conspiracy against the public, or in some contrivance to raise prices" and that the interest of the employers of capital "is always in some respects different from, and even opposite to, that of the public,"[35] it is clear that preserving and protecting competition and the free market must ever be a concern of government. As Skinner has noted, Smith recognized that the functions of the state "are quite indispensable."[36]

The Wealth of Nations is concerned with *effective* and not merely "formal" economic justice and liberty. Smith exposes and aims to reform all those public policies, institutions, laws and rules of taxation which, 1) help to create, encourage or sustain enterprises or incorporations of capital or labor which can escape the competitive pressures of the market place and impose an unjust and "absurd tax on their countrymen" through higher prices and profit, or 2) which effectively restrict access to certain types of employment and investments or new uses of capital and other factors of production, thereby preventing or inhibiting alternative goods, methods or processes from arising and competing with established ones.

It would therefore be erroneous to argue that *The Wealth of Nations* was only concerned with injustices arising from "legal" as distinguished from "market" monopolies or imperfections or that Smith proposed to accept oppressive or unjust practices provided only that they somehow originated in a competitive market situation. Furthermore, it must be remembered that, for Smith, the system of natural liberty practically excluded the enormous and entrenched concentrations of economic power and resources made possible by the corporate form; it did not have "regulatory" agencies involved in sustaining high prices and profits and inhibiting change, and it was open to almost unrestricted foreign trade and competition. Very few industries, in these circumstances, could attain the kind of market position which would enable them to oppress the public. Nevertheless, injustices, whatever their origins, can only continue where the law permits and protects them. Since government has the responsibility of "protecting, as far as possible, every member of the society from the injustice or oppression of every other member of it,"[37] government is obliged to prevent, correct or ameliorate economically oppressive practices and institutions.

Jacob Viner and other scholars have recognized that Adam Smith made many "exceptions" to his general argument for economic liberty. Spengler has commented that "Smith's definition of what the state could do was quite elastic and his list of specific tasks which the state should perform was rather long."[38] Viner explains this by suggesting that, at times, "Smith conveniently forgot the principle [of natural liberty] and went beyond the limits set in his formal discussion to the proper activities of government."[39] Spengler more accurately points out that because Smith's thoughts on the tasks of government are not all in one place and because his emphasis was on the virtues of economic liberty, he "left the impression of circumscribing the role of government even more than he in fact proposed [a] misleading impression which set the tone for subsequent writers."[40] The implications and significance of the specific tasks assigned to government and of these exceptions to natural liberty in *The Wealth of Nations* are best understood as related not to Smith's forgetfulness, eclecticism or elasticity of principle but to a consistent vision of a just and desireable economic order comprehensive enough so that "considerable controlling duties given to the State"[41] could have a natural and constructive place within it.

Since "consumption is the sole end and purpose of all production; and the interest of the producer ought to be attended to, only so far as it may be necessary for promoting that of the consumer,"[42] one principal guide for the role of

government within the system of natural liberty that seemed
to have a prominent place in Smith's mind was that of protecting the consumer. *The Wealth of Nations* argues that the
release of productive energies and resources brought about by
greater competition and a freer market would serve the
consumer and help him to exert a "real and effectual discipline"
over the producers in a way which "restrains his frauds and
corrects his negligence."[43] But in asserting that economic
liberty was necessary to protect the consumer, Smith did not
argue that it was in all cases sufficient. He was aware of the
problem of recognizing and dealing with bad workmanship
and inferior quality goods. The exposure of such articles to
public sale, he maintained, was often "the effect of fraud"
and he suggested that "regulations are necessary to prevent
this abuse," citing with approval such examples as the sterling
mark on silver and quality stamps upon linen and woolen
cloth as giving the purchaser "much greater security."[44] Where
the public could easily be fooled by appearances, government
should require that goods be labelled and information provided
so that persons would know what they are purchasing. Legislation directed toward aiding intelligent consumer choice and
the prevention of misleading representation and fraud was not
viewed as an unwarranted interference with just liberty.

Smith's discussion of banking practices in Book 2 of *The
Wealth of Nations* illustrates some of the concerns which he
thought justified public intervention and regulation of certain
aspects of commerce and production. The unrestrained liberty
of issuing very small denomination bank notes or paper
currencies encouraged the founding of a great many tiny and
financially insecure banks whose "frequent bankruptcies. . .
occasion a very inconsiderable inconveniency, and sometimes
even a very great calamity, to many poor people who had received
their notes in payment."[45] He therefore proposed that bankers
be prohibited from issuing such currency notes, even if "all his
neighbors are willing to accept them," though "it may be said"
that this "is a manifest violation of that natural liberty which it is
the proper business of law, not to infringe, but to support."

Such regulations may, no doubt, be considered as in some respect a violation of natural liberty. But those exertions of the natural liberty of a few individuals, which might endanger the security of the whole society, are and ought to be, restrained by the laws of all governments; of the most free, as well as of the most despotical. The obligation of building party walls, in order to prevent the communication of fire, is a violation of natural liberty exactly of the same kind with the regulations of the banking trade which are here proposed.[46]

These are only a few examples of Smith's recognition that, whatever the fundamental desirability of encouraging economic self-expression, the pursuit of individual and group interest did not always spontaneously result in morally or socially acceptable consequences. Provision of appropriate legal remedies for injury and an "exact" and "impartial" administration of justice in the economic order are also essential functions of government in Smith's paradigm. Without proper legal remedies or when the administration of justice was corrupted, a just economic liberty could not be realized. An "unqualified adherence to the principles of *caveat emptor* was apparently not a necessary implication of Smith's laissez faire doctrine."[47]

Another important area of government activity, namely, appropriate public works and institutions, is justified by reasons quite different from those which aim to correct or restrain the defects or "excesses" of self-interested endeavors. Adam Smith never refers to the legitimate provision of public services as involving "violations of natural liberty." On the contrary, he argues that public authority must undertake the task of providing those highly desirable services which the free market cannot or does not provide. Government is responsible for

erecting and maintaining those public institutions and those public works, which though they may be in the highest degree advantageous to a great society, are however, of such a nature, that the profit could never repay the expence to any individual or small number of individuals, and which it therefore cannot be expected that any individual or small number of individuals should erect or maintain.[48]

When certain services which are also in the public interest cannot be financed by the contribution of those who are most immediately benefitted, "the deficiency must in most cases be

made up by the general contribution of the whole society."[49]
Smith is not hostile to public institutions, but he seems to
believe that public works and services must be defended on
moral as well as utilitarian grounds; they ought to be so clearly
necessary and desirable that citizens "without injustice" may
be required or coerced into paying for them. While his views
of the role of government on this question are not dogmatic,
they place a much heavier burden on the moral wisdom of
public authority than is commonly appreciated.

Smith proposed two distinct though overlapping principles
as the basis for public services. One countenanced social overhead capital or public works for the primary purpose of facilitating commerce and industry. Transportation and communications facilities, roads, bridges, canals etc., classic examples of
this type of public enterprise, were "no doubt beneficial to the
whole society, and may, therefore, without any injustice, be
defrayed by the general contribution of the whole society."[50]
His primary concern respecting this category of publicly
financed facilities was that, as much as possible those who use
them ought "to pay for the maintenance of those public works
exactly in proportion to the wear and tear which they occasion
to them. It seems scarcely possible to invent a more equitable
way of maintaining such works."[51] The necessity for a cost-
benefit relationship would also help to ensure that public works
were built where they were the most needed and valuable to
the community. A concern for equity as well as efficiency
guides his entire discussion of the role of government in providing social overhead capital, including the problems of appropriate
management for public enterprises and the question of local
finance and control.

Smith's defense of a second type of public service reflects
an awareness in regard to certain socially desirable institutions,
that those who are most immediately benefitted by them may
be too poor to pay for them. The community, for example,
has an interest in seeing that all children obtain a certain level
of education. Every society, Smith maintained, requires an
appropriate kind of moral and intellectual character in its

members. But in civilized societies, economic growth, which is necessarily connected with increasing division of labor and specialization, tends to confine the skills of working people "to a few very simple operations" and therefore to "benumb the understanding" of the laboring poor. In developing societies, the "invisible hand" apparently does not produce a requisite level of moral and intellectual vigor. On the contrary, it tends to produce large numbers of men "without the proper use of the intellectual faculties" and therefore "deformed in an essential part of the character of human nature."[52]

In Smith's view, the "attention of government" was necessary if individuals were to be protected against the moral and intellectual stultification resulting from a premature introduction to labor. His thoughts on public education for children perhaps best exemplify some of the general criteria which he believed should guide public provision of services in a just economy. First, there must be an identified need of uncommon importance which is not being fulfilled because it is beyond the means of those immediately benefitted. Second, public authority should not undermine the freedom and ability of families or individuals to provide for their own needs in their own way and with their own means, to the extent possible. Third, public money should not be employed to displace or compete unfairly with private institutions and services. Fourth, private and public means and controls should be combined whenever possible. For example, even in publicly provided schools, parents should be responsible for some direct payment to the school in order to encourage the diligence of teachers and furnish an avenue of influence for the parents.[53]

But perhaps the most important aspect of Smith's discussion of education is the implication that government is responsible for correcting or offsetting the deleterious consequences of commercial society when such consequences derive from the very nature of a complex, specialized and interdependent free market economic order. The significance of this idea for guiding the organization and regulation of certain functions of government within the system of natural liberty, i.e., for harmonizing to a greater degree the elements of justice, liberty, and equality, has been almost entirely overlooked. Smith emphasized certain harmful tendencies resulting from industrial progress not to condemn commercial society and the division of labor, but to urge public attention to remedying its shortcomings. In light of Smith's ideas on the role of government within the system of economic liberty, as well as his emphasis on considerations of justice which so pervade *The Wealth of Nations,* it is hard to imagine that he would object to a vigorous involvement of public authority in such problems of modern economic life as unemployment, health, pollution, etc., though he might well object to many particular methods of amelioration as unjust, unwise or inefficient.

ANTI-COLONIALISM

Adam Smith's opposition and hostility to colonialism and imperialism is of particular significance in this bicentennial year of 1976. *The Wealth of Nations* was the first great anti-colonialist and anti-imperialist tract, in the modern sense of those terms, referring to that particular combination of unwelcome and oppressive authority and economic exploitation imposed by some states on other territories or peoples. This is evident not only in Smith's critique of mercantilism, the theoretical basis of seventeenth- and eighteenth-century colonialism, but in his direct attack on the morality as well as the economics of colonial imperialism. The anti-colonialist theme is an important part of his lengthy chapter on colonies in Book 4. This theme emerges in the first book and persists until the very last page of Smith's work. Yet his real stature as an anti-colonialist thinker is little known. Marxist-Leninist analysis is actually a latecomer to the school of anti-colonialism and it has preempted and obfuscated much of the subject in part because its powerful antecedents in Smith's political economy have been ignored and its implications unappreciated. Had those who were concerned with international economic injustice paid due attention to his analysis, it might have been much more difficult to establish the erroneous view that

modern imperialisms are expressions of economic liberty
rather than negations of it.

The twin themes of Smith's liberal anti-colonialism are
injustice and disadvantage. Colonialism was unjust and harmful both to the dependent peoples and to the colonizing
nations. It was commercially destructive and financially
disastrous. *The Wealth of Nations* provided a detailed critique
of British attempts to restrict and exploit the American
economies. Under these unjust and absurd policies, higher
rates of profit took precedence over the national interest. The
advantages which colonialism procured to a "single order of
men" was "in many different ways hurtful to the general
interest of the country."

> To found a great empire for the sole purpose of raising up a people of
> customers may at first sight appear a project fit only for a nation of shop-
> keepers. It is, however, a project altogether unfit for a nation of shop-
> keepers; but extremely fit for a nation whose government is influenced
> by shopkeepers. Such statesmen, and such statesmen only, are capable
> of fancying that they will find some advantage in employing the blood
> and treasure of their fellow-citizens to found and maintain such an
> empire.[54]

A just economy does not buy special privileges abroad for
capital owners and investors with the "blood and treasure"
of its citizens.

Although he assessed the net impact of British exploitation
of North American as "not . . . very hurtful," because due to
cheap land and the very high wage rates of labor in the colonies
they could import almost all the manufactured goods they
needed cheaper than they could produce them for themselves,
Smith condemned British policies as "unjust" and "impertinent
badges of slavery imposed upon them, without any sufficient
reason, by the groundless jealousy of the merchants and manufacturers of the mother country."

> To prohibit a great people . . . from making all that they can of every
> part of their own produce, or from employing their stock and industry
> in the way that *they* judge most advantageous, is a manifest violation
> of the most sacred rights of mankind.[55]

The burning issue of the American colonies provoked the anti-colonialist insistence that only justice, liberty, equality and consent were an acceptable basis for a resolution of the conflict between Britain and her contentious offspring. In proposals which illustrate a radical imagination and insight, Smith argued that Britain ought to seek genuine union with her North American colonies, whose leaders were, at that very time, "contriving a new form of government for an extensive empire, which, they flatter themselves, will become, and which, indeed, seems very likely to become, one of the greatest and most formidable that ever was in the world."[56]

There is not the least probability that the British constitution would be hurt by the union of Great Britain with her colonies. That constitution, on the contrary, would be completed by it, and seems to be imperfect without it.[57]

The principle of representation would make such a union possible. Even under taxation with representation, however, the Americans would undoubtedly be concerned about being neglected, given their distance from the seat of government. Since representation ought to be in proportion to taxation, this distance would not very likely be of long duration.

Such has hitherto been the rapid progress of that country in wealth, population and improvement, that in the course of little more than a century, perhaps, the produce of American might exceed that of British taxation. The seat of empire would than naturally remove itself to that part of the empire which contributed most to the general defence and support of the whole.[58]

Such was Adam Smith's view of the best solution to one instance of colonialism; a first "British Commonwealth" based on constitutional liberty, representation and economic freedom.

In a preview of what was to be one of the most important arguments for real union to be found many years later in the *Federalist Papers,* Smith contended that the North American colonies

would in point of happiness and tranquility, gain considerably by a union with Great Britain. It would at least deliver them from those rancorous and virulent factions which are inseperable from small democracies, and which have so frequently divided the affections of their people, and disturbed the tranquility of their governments, in their form so nearly democratical.[59]

A union of Great Britain and her colonies might indeed be difficult but the problems were not insurmountable. The greatest ones "perhaps arise, not from the nature of things, but from the prejudices and opinions of the people on this and on the other side of the Atlantic."[60]

The force of these prejudices led Smith to propose a second equally dramatic solution: total independence.

Great Britain should voluntarily give up all authority over her colonies, and leave them to elect their own magistrates, to enact their own laws, and to make peace and war as they might think proper.[61]

He was not at all hopeful of the adoption of this solution by his government or fellow citizens, however, for he believed that due to national pride and the prospective loss of opportunities for position, wealth and distinction "no nation ever voluntarily gave up the dominion of any province, how troublesome soever it might be to govern it, and how small soever the revenue which it afforded might be in proportion to the expense which it occasioned."[62] Nevertheless, justice and wisdom dictated either voluntary union or independence. The imposition of authority meant hostilities between the colonies and "the best of all mother countries."

For Smith, the modern idea of colonialism violated the precepts of natural liberty and justice. Colonial relationships invited oppressive policies and laws and were in fact an enormous political, military and financial burden to the community, however profitable they might be to certain political and business interests. Great Britain "derives nothing but loss from the dominion she assumes over her colonies." The economics of colonialism were absurd. Britain, Smith asserted, was, "perhaps, since the world began, the only state which, as it has extended its empire, has only increased its expense without once augmenting its resources."[63] The British people ought not to support and could ill afford such an "empire." Either it should be reconstituted on a more just and equitable basis or the "golden dream" of empire abandoned and Britain should "endeavour to accomodate her future views and designs to the real mediocrity of her circumstances."[64]

The Wealth of Nations represents a "radical" political-economics; radical in the sense of being grounded on the moral roots of social relationships and radical in the sense of rooting economy in a political-moral context. Like most classics of political and economic philosophy, Smith's treatise has the virtue of combining the pursuit of truth with the pursuit of just reform. *The Wealth of Nations* is not the last word on the just economy, but it is one of the first. The nature of a just economic order remains the central question of political economy.

It is a paradox in contemporary understanding that Marx, who never speaks of justice and injustice, but of science and the laws of motion and development, is everywhere known for the passionately moral character of his language and thought. Smith, on the other hand, who acknowledges the normative problem of justice as central to social analysis, is usually thought to represent an economic science bereft of moral concern.

Nevertheless, Smith's principles of political economy are fundamentally moral principles. They are favorable neither to robbers nor to barons. They are basically concerned with enhancing the possibilities for individual and societal development, minimizing class privilege, ensuring that governmental activity serves the public interest, protecting those unjustly harmed by modern economic life and preventing and rectifying exploitative relationships between people and nations.

NOTES

1. References to Adam Smith's writings are to the following editions: *The Wealth of Nations*, Cannan ed., (New York, Modern Library, 1937) cited hereafter as WN; *The Theory of Moral Sentiments* (New York, A.M. Kelley, 1966) cited hereafter as TMS; and *Lectures on Justice, Police, Revenue and Arms*, Cannan ed., (New York, A.M. Kelley, 1964), cited hereafter as *Lectures*.

2. TMS, p. 31.

3. TMS, p. 125.

4. TMS, p. 130.

5. TMS, p. 114.

6. WN, p. 628.

7. WN, p. 572.

8. WN, p. 141.

9. TMS, p. 194.

10. TMS, p. 343.

11. WN, p. 651.

12. Glenn R. Morrow, "Adam Smith; Moralist and Philosopher," in J.M. Clark et al., *Adam Smith, 1776-1926* (New York: A.M. Kelley, 1966), p. 167.

13. J. Ralph Lindgren, *The Social Philosophy of Adam Smith* (The Hague: Martinus Nijhoff, 1973), pp. 54-55.

14. Robert Nozick, *Anarchy, State and Utopia* (New York: Basic Books, 1974), see esp. pp. 152-53, 208.

15. WN, p. 392.

16. WN, p. 363.

17. WN, p. 699-700.

18. WN, p. 699.

19. Karl Marx, *Early Writings*, T.B. Bottomore, ed., (New York: McGraw-Hill, 1964), pp. 147-48.

20. WN, p. lvii.

21. WN, p. 30.

22. WN, p. 249.

23. WN, p. 122.

24. WN, p. 670.

25. P.J. McNulty, "Adam Smith's Concept of Labor," *Journal of the History of Ideas 34* (July-September 1973): 346.

26. WN, p. 64.

27. R. Heilbroner, "Decline and Decay in *The Wealth of Nations*," *Journal of the History of Ideas 34* (April-June 1973): 260.

28. WN, p. 389.

29. WN, p. 259.

30. WN, pp. 86, 260, 271.

31. WN, p. 566.

32. *Lectures*, p. 162.

33. WN, p. 12.

34. WN, p. 437-38.

35. WN, p. 128, 250.

36. Andrew Skinner, *Adam Smith and the Role of the State* (Glascow: University of Glascow Press, 1974), p. 8.

37. WN, p. 699.

38. J.J. Spengler, "The Problem of Order in Economic Affairs," *Southern Economic Journal 15* (July 1948): 16.

39. Jacob Viner, "Adam Smith and Laissez-Faire," in J.M. Clark et al., *Adam Smith*, p. 150.

40. Spengler, *Problem of Order,* p. 161.
41. A.L. Macfie, *The Individual in Society* (London: Allen and Unwin, 1967), p. 77.
42. WN, p. 625.
43. WN, p. 129.
44. WN, p. 122.
45. WN, p. 307.
46. WN, p. 308.
47. Viner, *Adam Smith,* p. 145.
48. WN, p. 681.
49. WN, p. 768.
50. WN, p. 767.
51. WN, p. 683.
52. WN, p. 740.
53. WN, p. 716-40.
54. WN, p. 579.
55. WN, p. 549, my emphasis.
56. WN, p. 588.
57. WN, p. 589.
58. WN, p. 590.
59. WN, p. 897.
60. WN, p. 589.
61. WN, p. 581.
62. WN, p. 582.
63. WN, p. 586.
64. WN, p. 900.

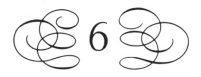

Smith Versus Marx on Business Morality and the Social Interest

Based on 6,200+ reviews

William J. Baumol
PRINCETON UNIVERSITY AND NEW YORK UNIVERSITY

I BELIEVE that among those who know *The Wealth of Nations* mostly by repute there is widespread misinterpretation of its central message about the roles of capitalists and capitalism. The book is neither a tract that opposes all forms of government intervention in the workings of the free market,[1] nor does it dedicate itself to the praise of virtuous intentions and high moral standards of the capitalists. On the contrary, Smith's basic position is that in the operation of the economy there is nothing so untrustworthy as the businessman's good intentions. The economy in *The Wealth of Nations* is populated by a group of individuals intent on pursuit of their own interests, with little concern over the resulting damage to the welfare of others, and businessmen are second to none in their disregard of the public interest.

The basic virtue of the market mechanism, when it is operated without monopolistic restrictions or *inappropriate* governmental interference, is that it not only places a rein upon such selfish behavior, but that it achieves even more, turning pursuit of self-interest into an instrument for the promotion of the general welfare. In this mechanism *disregard for the interests of others plays a crucial role;* without it, that is, if the conscience of businessmen were to replace their pursuit of personal gain, the interests of society might not be served nearly as well.

In contrast, Marx's view is that the capitalist as an individual is neither inherently good nor evil, but the inevitable product of historical circumstances which, on the one hand, make him the progenitor of progress over medieval stagnation and, on the other, the destined but transitory exploiter of the working class. Thus it is paradoxical, but entirely consistent with their central purposes, that the book widely considered to be the charter document of the free enterprise system repeatedly attacks the ethics of the merchants and manufacturers, while the volumes that have become the manifesto of the opponents of capitalism do not concern themselves with the capitalist's personal morality.

In sum, it will be my objective to show that while to Marx the capitalist is the product of the historical process, that is, the creation of the capitalist stage of history, to Smith the capitalist system is a mechanism designed, apparently by divine providence, to curb man's inherent selfishness and, indeed, to put it to work for the general good. These are among the central messages of *Capital* and of *The Wealth of Nations,* and so the two authors' contrasting views on the personal morality of capitalists are not incidental quirks of the writers but a direct reflection of their basic views.

1. SMITH ON BUSINESS ETHICS

Though most of them are quite familiar, a selection of some more notable quotations giving Smith's views on the ethics of businessmen bear repetition because readers who have not seen them recently may be struck by their force and consistency.

Proceeding more or less in their order of appearance in the book, we start with one in which Smith accuses businessmen of heaping upon labor the blame for high prices, and studiously ignoring their own contribution to the problem:

Our merchants and master-manufacturers complain much of the bad effects of high wages in raising the price, and thereby lessening the sale of their goods both at home and abroad. They say nothing concerning the bad effects of high profits. They are silent with regard to the pernicious effects of their own gains. They complain only of those of other people. (p. 98)

However, it is not only labor that suffers from the weakness of the capitalists' scruples, and Smith tells us that the public, as a body, is also a likely victim:

People of the same trade seldom meet together, even for merriment and diversion, but the conversation ends in a conspiracy against the public, or in some contrivance to raise prices. (p. 128)

According to Smith, businessmen as a group try to exercise economic power over their countrymen by restraining trade and monopolizing the domestic markets:

. . .merchants and manufacturers, who being collected into towns, and accustomed to that exclusive corporation spirit which prevails in them, naturally endeavour to obtain against all their countrymen, the same exclusive privilege which they generally possess against the inhabitants of their respective towns. They accordingly seem to have been the original inventors of those restraints upon the importation of foreign goods, which secure to them the monopoly of the home market. (p. 249)

Not only do the capitalists restrain trade, but they seek to deceive the public into believing that high domestic prices somehow serve the general interest:

In every country it always is and must be the interest of the great body of the people to buy whatever they want of those who sell it cheapest. The proposition is so very manifest, that it seems ridiculous to take any pains to prove it; nor could it ever have been called in question, had not the interested sophistry of merchants and manufacturers confounded the common sense of mankind. Their interest is, in this respect, directly opposite to that of the great body of the people. (p. 461)

Indeed, the influence of capitalists upon foreign trade favors impoverishment of other countries, and undermines international tranquility:

. . .nations have been taught that their interest consisted in beggaring all their neighbours. Each nation has been made to look with an invidious eye upon the prosperity of all the nations with which it trades, and to consider their gain as its own loss. Commerce, which ought naturally to be, among nations, as among individuals, a bond of union and friendship, has become the most fertile source of discord and animosity. The capricious ambition of kings and ministers has not, during the present and the preceding century, been more fatal to the repose of Europe, than the impertinent jealousy of merchants and manufacturers. The violence and injustice of the rulers of mankind is an ancient evil, for which, I am afraid, the nature of human affairs can scarce admit of a remedy. But the mean rapacity, the monopolizing spirit of merchants and manufacturers, who neither are, nor ought to be, the rulers of mankind, though it cannot perhaps be corrected, may very easily be prevented from disturbing the tranquility of anybody but themselves. (p. 460)

It is not surprising, then, that Smith has little use for a government of businessmen:

The government of an exclusive company of merchants is, perhaps, the worst of all governments for any country whatever. (p. 537)

In sum, there should be no doubt about Smith's strong distrust of the ethics of businessmen and their dedication to their social responsibilities.

2. THE INVISIBLE HAND AND BUSINESS VIRTUE

We have no reason to attribute Smith's vehemence to personal animosity. On the contrary, John Rae in his biography tells us that Smith befriended the Glasgow merchants and manufacturers and apparently learned a great deal from them about current business practices. (Rae pp. 90-95) There is no hint that he had any unpleasant dealings with businessmen even in his role as collector of customs, a post Smith held in Edinburgh for the last twelve years of his life, and one which he seems to have taken very seriously.[2]

A much more straightforward explanation is provided in *The Wealth of Nations*. One of the central themes of the book, which is emphasized from its very beginning, is that it is a serious mistake to entrust the economic welfare of society to the good intentions of *any* man. What better way to emphasize this point than to remind us repeatedly of the moral frailty of the group most likely to acquire power over the economy.

In a celebrated passage at the beginning of Chapter 2, Smith admonishes us not to rely on anyone's good intentions for the benefits we hope to obtain from the economy:

...man has almost constant occasion for the help of his brethren, and it is in vain for him to expect it from their benevolence only. He will be more likely to prevail if he can interest their self-love in his favour, and shew them that it is for their own advantage to do for him what he requires of them. Whoever offers to another a bargain of any kind, proposes to do this. Give me that which I want, and you shall have this which you want, is the meaning of every such offer; and it is in this manner that we obtain from one another the far greater part of those good offices which we stand in need of. It is not from the benevolence of the butcher, the brewer, or the baker, that we expect our dinner, but from their regard to their own interest. We address ourselves, not to their humanity but to their self-love, and never talk to them of our own necessities but of their advantages. (p. 14)

The passage already suggests the view that reaches its most dramatic expression in the invisible hand passage—the doctrine that self-interest, properly channeled, is a much more reliable protector of the public interest than is any arrangement dependent upon the personal morality of the decision maker. This is the central message of the paragraph on the invisible hand. There, in some of his most telling phrases, Smith tells us how wary we must be of the businessman's commitment to his "social responsibilities":

As every individual endeavours as much as he can...to employ his capital...that its produce may be of the greatest value; every individual necessarily labours to render the annual revenue of the society as great as he can. He generally, indeed, neither intends to promote the public interest, nor knows how much he is promoting it...by directing that industry in such a manner as its produce may be of the greatest value, he intends only his own gain, and he is in this, as in many other cases, led by an invisible hand to promote an end which was no part of his intention. Nor is it always the worse for the society that it was no part of it. By pursuing his own interest he frequently promotes that of the society more effectually than when he really intends to promote it. *I have never known much good done by those who affected to trade for the public good. It is an affectation, indeed, not very common among merchants, and very few words need be employed in dissuading them from it.* (p. 423, my italics)

The point in all this is *not* just that individual virtue, both that of businessmen *and of others*,[3] is untrustworthy, but that there is available a better means, the market mechanism, in which society *can* put its trust. The market mechanism does not merely curb human frailty and prevent its unfortunate effects. Rather it turns matters about completely, putting that frailty to work in the service of the general welfare. He goes so far as to assert that it succeeds in making the individual do "as much as he can" to promote the general interest.

Moreover, it is no accident that the businessman seeks to subvert this beneficent process. The market mechanism, and its competitive instrument, is a harsh taskmaker—it can impose painful pressures upon the business firm.[4] That is precisely why management can be expected to use every means it can to subvert the process, to conspire against the public, to seek to replace competition by monopoly [which removes from them the pressures for efficiency of operation—(p. 447)].

3. THE INVISIBLE HAND AS INSTRUMENT OF PROVIDENCE

We are inclined nowadays to treat the invisible hand as mere metaphor; but there is some reason to believe that in Smith's mind it was much more than that.[5] Though he occasionally found himself at odds with representatives of the religious establishment (particularly over his friendship with Hume, the skeptic, who took great pleasure in baiting the church), Smith was a theist who believed deeply in the role of God. (Rae, pp. 129, 429-30) In *The Theory of Moral Sentiments,* the Deity is involved frequently and plays an important part in the discussion. In particular, there is one passage (not otherwise germaine to our discussion) in which the invisible hand makes its appearance, and there seems little question that at that point it is the hand of God:

[The rich] are led *by an invisible hand* to make nearly the same distribution of the necessaries of life, which would have been made, had the earth been divided into equal portions among all its inhabitants, and thus without intending it, advance the interest of the society, and offer a means to the multiplication of the species. *When Providence divided the earth among a few lordly masters, it neither forgot nor abandoned those who seemed to have been left out in the partition.* (p. 163, my italics)[6]

Now, in a relatively early paper, Viner points out that Adam Smith of *The Theory of Moral Sentiments* does not always hold the same views as the author of *The Wealth of Nations.*[7] However, that does not preclude the possibility that the invisible hand of the two volumes was the same.[8]

In his earlier discussion Viner maintained that "the emphasis in *The Theory of Moral Sentiments,* upon a benevolent deity as the author and guide of nature is almost, though not quite, completely absent in *The Wealth of Nations*" [1927, p. 221]. However, by 1966 he seems to have changed his mind on this score:

Modern professors of economics and of ethics operate in disciplines which have been secularized to the point where the religious elements and implications which once were an integral part of them have been painstakingly eliminated . . . [H]owever, I am obliged to insist that Adam Smith's system of thought, including his economics, is not intelligible if one disregards the role he assigns in it to the theological elements, to the 'invisible hand.' " (11, pp. 81-82)

The point in all this is that it suggests an interpretation of the free enterprise system as an instrument of the Deity designed to curb the frailty of humanity. It is, as it were, a second-best solution, which not merely can undo the mischief that might be produced by the avarice that has afflicted humanity since the fall of man. Rather, it turns that avarice against itself, transforming it into a prime instrument of public virtue. It is a device adopted by a very practical Providence to deal with the unfortunate but very real weakness of human character.

However, whether or not God plays the role in the analysis that I have surmised, the general point seems valid enough. To Smith of *The Wealth of Nations* man in general, and the businessman in particular, is morally weak and untrustworthy. Some rules of the game must therefore be instituted to protect society from the individual. The free enterprise system, whatever the instrument of its design, is a superb mechanism for the purpose. That is the essence of the relationship between the businessman and the free enterprise system as envisaged by Smith.

4. THE MARXIAN INVERSION

It is noteworthy that in the Marxian analysis the relative moral positions of the businessman and business enterprise are nearly reversed. Taken as a person, the entrepreneur is not particularly evil (or particularly virtuous). Not that Marx approves of business behavior. One example will suffice to dispell any doubts on that score:

. . . the prodigality of the capitalist never possesses the bona-fide character of the open-handed feudal lord's prodigality, but, on the contrary, has always lurking behind it the most sordid avarice and the most anxious calculation. [The early capitalists] enriched themselves chiefly by robbing the parents, whose children were bound as apprentices to them: the parents paid a high premium, while the apprentices were starved. (*Capital,* vol. I, p. 651)

Yet to Marx, an historical materialist, the capitalist did evil deeds not because he was born or raised to be a moral cripple but because the material circumstances left him no choice:

And so far only is the necessity for his own transitory existence implied in the transitory necessity for the capitalist mode of production. . . . Fanatically bent on making value expand itself, he ruthlessly forces the human race to produce for production's sake; hc thus forces the development of the productive powers of society, and creates those material conditions, which alone can form the real basis of a higher form of society, a society in which the full and free development of every individual forms the ruling principle. Only as personified capital is the capitalist respectable. As such, he shares with the miser the passion for wealth as wealth. *But that which in the miser is a mere idiosyncrasy, is, in the capitalist, the effect of the social mechanism, of which he is but one of the wheels.* (vol. I, p. 649, my italics)

That is to say, historical forces give the capitalists no choice, be they as morally pure and discerning as Friedrich Engels, the manufacturer of Barmen and Manchester. Had the accident of inheritance reversed the roles of a particular proletarian and a particular capitalist, the former would readily have fallen into the role of exploiter and the latter would have assumed that of victim.

The doctrine of historical materialism is often misunderstood as naive economic interpretation—as the view that every human action is to be considered the product of careful calculation of self-interest. Perhaps this may be true of some recent writings by *non*-Marxist economists on the economics of crime, race discrimination and marriage, but it certainly is *not* true of Marx. In his historical materialism economic influences usually exert final control, but often in a subtle manner and at second remove. Human personality does play an important role in history, but the scope for its action is provided by historical circumstances, and the personality itself is heavily influenced by historical conditions.[9]

Moreover, in different historical circumstances, the social implications of the capitalist's role will vary correspondingly. Thus, Marx emphasized consistently that the capitalist was not always the embodiment of reaction. From *The Communist Manifesto* (1847) to *The Critique of the Gotha Program* (1875) Marx reiterated that "the bourgeoisie is...a revolutionary class—as the bearer of large-scale industry—relatively to the feudal lords and the lower middle class, who desire to maintain all social positions that are the creation of obsolete modes of production." (*Critique of the Gotha Program,* Comment 4).

Thus, in Marx, the capitalist, with all his crimes, is not the product of a warped morality, but of a set of circumstances that give him no choice. In Smith he is an inherently immoral man whom the capitalist system is designed to restrain. In Marx he is neither inherently moral nor immoral. It is the stage of history that brings capital (rather than the capitalist) into the world "dripping from head to foot, from every pore, with blood and dirt." (vol. I, p. 834)

CONCLUSIONS

In summary, the difference in the treatment of the capitalist by the two writers reflects both the difference in their view of history and the difference in the purpose of their major works. To Smith even "the early and rude state of society" in which labor is the only scarce resource is a sort of primitive free enterprise system, albeit one without capitalists or landlords.

For it is the market mechanism that presumably drives relative prices of deer and beaver into equality with the relative amounts of labor required to hunt them. Thus, Smith's economic history is a progression from a simple to a complex market system, but it is a history in which the institution is permanent, and its workings can be permanently beneficent if they are not subjected to unwise interference which unchains the selfishness of humanity and permits it to do harm to the community rather than working for the public benefit.

To Marx on the other hand, the capitalist system is a transitory phenomenon, and like every other stage in history it makes its people what they are. The capitalist is not without his virtues—he is a Schumpeterian entrepreneur[10] to be admired for his dynamism of creativity, but he is also a ruthless exploiter. But neither his virtues nor his vices are to be attributed to him alone, for they are ultimately to be ascribed to the stage of society that has created his role. His activities can be redirected to serve the general welfare more effectively, and he himself can be made into a better man, but this can be done only by another historical stage, the communist society that was Marx's goal.[11]

NOTES

1. Besides Smith's long discussion, in Book V, of the appropriate general functions of government as the provision of national defense, the administration of justice and the supply of public services, he recognizes explicitly the role of externalities and the justification they provide for governmental intervention. In a passage proposing restrictions on banking practices of which economists were recently reminded by Lord Robbins, Smith wrote:

those exertions of the natural liberty of a few individuals, which might endanger the security of the whole society, are, and ought to be, restrained by the laws of all governments; of the most free, as well as of the most despotical. The obligation of building party walls, in order to prevent the communication of fire, is a violation of natural liberty, exactly of the same kind with the regulations of the banking trade which are here proposed (p. 308).

2. Indeed, the only person with whom Smith clearly seems to have been involved in a personal clash was Samuel Johnson. Their dislike was apparently mutual and instantanous, though matters seem eventually to have healed. See Rae pp. 35, 154-58, 366.

3. Thus recall Smith's delightful discussion of the dangers of paying university teachers stipends, that do not vary with the number of students they are able to attract, as in eighteenth-century Oxford where "the greater part of the public professors have, for these many years, given up altogether even the pretense of teaching." (p. 718) Note also Smith's quotation of Hume's plea for an exception in the case of churchmen who will be led, if they are paid by results to seek to attract parishioners by appealing to "superstition, folly, and delusion. Each ghostly practitioner, in order to render himself more precious and sacred in the eyes of his retainers [will pay] no regard . . . to truth, morals, or decency in the doctrines inculcated." (p. 743) Thus the market mechanism *can* sometimes backfire.

4. "Their [merchants'] competition might perhaps ruin some of themselves; but to take care of this is the business of the parties concerned, and it may safely be trusted to their discretion. It can never hurt either the consumer, or the producer; on the contrary, it must tend to make the retailers both sell cheaper and buy dearer . . ." (p. 342-43)

5. This section obviously relies heavily on Viner [10]. However, its conclusions are not quite the same as Viner's, as will be noted presently.

6. Quoted in Viner [1927] p. 219.

7. For example, the rejection in the latter volume of benevolence as a reliable source of public welfare is in direct conflict with the basic theme of the former.

8. Perhaps it is suggestive that in the famous passage in *The Wealth of Nations* Smith says that the individual "is . . . led *by* an invisible hand" not "led *as though* by an invisible hand." (my italics)

9. See e.g., G.V.Plekhanov, *The Role of the Individual in History*. Plekhanov discusses at length various noteworthy historical cases to show that even the most accidental events assume their importance from current historical (economic) conditions, and that the long-run influence of such accidental events is usually minimal. Thus, for example he points out "In 1789, Davout, Désaix, Marmont and MacDonald were subalterns; Bernadotte was a sergeant-major; Hoche, Marceau, Lefebre, Pichegru, Ney, Massena, Murat and Soult were non-commissioned officers; Augereau was a fencing master; Lannes was a dyer; Gouvion Saint-Cyr was an actor; Jourdan was a peddler, Bessièrs was a barber; Brune was a compositor; Joubert and Junot were law students; Kleber was an architect; Martier did not see any military service until the Revolution.

"Had the old order continued to exist until our day it would never have occurred to any of us that in France, at the end of the last [the eighteenth] century, certain actors, compositors, barbers, dyers, lawyers, peddlers and fencing masters had been potential military geniuses." (p. 170)

Marx himself never discussed historical materialism at any length or very systematically. That is why so few quotations from Marx have been offered in this section.

10. The Schumpertian process is described in *Capital* very explicitly.

Thus note the following passage: "... the surplus-profit, which some individual capital may ordinarily realize in its particular sphere of production [is] due, aside from accidental deviations, to a reduction of the cost-price [which arises from] better methods of labor, new inventions, improved machinery, chemical secrets in manufacture, etc., in short, new and improved means of production and methods . . . a circumstance which is neutralized as soon as the exceptional method of production becomes general or is superseded by a still more developed one." (vol. III, pp. 754-55)

11. See *Critique of the Gotha Program,* Comment 3. cf. also *Grundrisse* p. 610 ff for Marx's view on the role and burdensomeness of labor under varying historical circumstances.

REFERENCES

1. Marx, Karl, *Capital* (Chicago: Charles H. Kerr and Co. vol. I (1906); vols. II and III (1909).

2. ———, *A Contribution to the Critique of Political Economy* N.I. Stone, trans. (Chicago: Charles H. Kerr and Co., 1904.)

3. ———, *Critique of the Gotha Program* (Moscow: Progress Publishing, 1937.)

4. *Grundrisse,* Martin Nicolaus, trans., ed. (Harmondsworth: Penguin Books, 1973.)

5. ——— and Friedrich Engels, *The Manifesto of the Communist Party.*

6. Plekhanov, G.V., *The Role of the Individual in History,* in Plekhanov, G.V., *Fundamental Problems of Marxism* (New York: International Publishers, 1969.)

7. Rae, John, *Life of Adam Smith* (London: Macmillan, 1895.)

8. Smith, Adam, *The Theory of Moral Sentiments* (Ward Lock & Co: London, n.d.)

9. ———, *The Wealth of Nations,* Cannan Edition (New York: The Modern Library, 1937.)

10. Viner, Jacob, "Adam Smith and Laissez Faire," *Journal of Political Economy* 35 (April 1927): 198-232, reprinted in Jacob Viner, *The Long View and The Short* (Glencoe, Illinois: Free Press, 1958) pp. 213-45.

11. ———, *The Role of Providence in the Social Order* (Philadelphia, American Philosophical Society, 1972.)

Adam Smith and the Industrial Revolution

Ronald Max Hartwell

OXFORD UNIVERSITY

I

Nineteen seventy-six is the bicentenary of an important intellectual event, the publication in London of Adam Smith's *An Inquiry into the Nature and Causes of the Wealth of Nations;* it is also the bicentenary of the rebellion of American colonies. 1776, indeed, was a vintage intellectual year in Britain, with the publication not only of *The Wealth of Nations,* but of the first volume of Edward Gibbon's *The Decline and Fall of the Roman Empire* (about the decay and dissolution of an ancient wealthy society), and of Jeremy Bentham's first publication, *A Fragment on Government* (in which he pronounced the utilitarian axiom that "it is the greatest happiness of the greatest number that is the measure of right and wrong"). And if for Britain the decade of the 1770s saw a successful political revolution abroad, at home it was, on conventional historical accounting, the decade of the beginnings of the industrial revolution. Americans should celebrate not only the rebellion, but also *The Wealth of Nations* and the industrial revolution, because Smith provided an enduring and effective rationale for that liberal political economy which allowed the expansion of nineteenth-century U.S.A.,[1] and because the industrial revolution was "the engine of growth" which, with its insatiable demand for cotton, did so much to stimulate American economic growth in the period up to an American industrial revolution.[2] Seventeen-seventy-six was the year also, alas, of the death of Smith's fellow Scot and great friend, David Hume, who had been anxiously awaiting the publications of *The Wealth of Nations* and *The Decline and Fall;* and since both books were published early in the year, Hume was able to read them in the spring before his expected death in late August. It was from the critically perceptive Hume that Smith received his first commendation: "Euge! Belle! Dear Mr. Smith—I am much pleased with your performance, and the perusal of it has taken me from a state of great anxiety. It was a work of so much expectation, by yourself, by your friends, and by the public, that I trembled for its appearance, but am now much relieved."[3]

Hume, however, even prompted by respect and affection for Smith, could hardly have imagined how practically successful *The Wealth of Nations* would be. It was in its influence on public policy undoubtedly the most influential book on economics ever written, challenged only by the massively destructive influence of *Das Kapital* of Karl Marx, and by the doubtfully beneficial, nco-mercantilist influence of *The General Theory of Employment, Interest and Money* of J.M. Keynes. Smith even had the satisfaction, in the words of his first biographer, Dugald Stewart, "to witness the practical influence of his writings on the commercial policy of his country."[4] By 1857 H.T. Buckle reckoned that *"The Wealth of Nations* . . . looking at its ultimate results, is probably the most important book that has ever been written, and is certainly the most valuable contribution ever made by a single man towards establishing the principles on which government should be based."[5] W. Gladstone, at a meeting in 1876 to celebrate the centennary of the publication of *The Wealth of Nations,* said that after Smith the economists had left only "the duty of propagating opinions which will have the effect of confining government within its proper province and preventing it from all manner of aggressions and intrusions upon the province of the free agency of the individual."[6] A. Toynbee, in his lectures in the 1880s, declared that *"The Wealth of Nations* and the steam engine...destroyed the old world and built a new one";[7] and J. Bonar, in Palgrave's *Dictionary* in 1894, wrote that "no economical treatise ever exerted greater political influence."[8] Certainly the publication of *The Wealth of Nations* coincided with the beginnings of the industrial revolution and an era of economic liberalism, and nineteenth-century writers had no doubt that the relationship was causal.[9] But even though he helped bring about the industrial revolution, did Smith realize that he was witnessing its beginnings?

II

German scholars use a phrase *Das Adam Smith Problem* to describe the apparent contradiction between the Smith of sympathy in *The Theory of Moral Sentiments* and the Smith of self-interest in *The Wealth of Nations*. And such is the range and complexity of Smith's works that the study of them by a host of scholars has conjured up a number of alleged problems: contradictions or paradoxes, failures to recognize the obvious, and obscurity or confusion in analysis.[10] Another and almost inevitable problem has been disagreement among scholars about what Smith really meant, and hence the necessity for other scholars to disentangle not Adam Smith's theories, but theories about Smith's theories. Undoubtedly the conflicting ethical positions taken by Smith in his two great published works has attracted the most attention. But if, as Jacob Viner has argued, the Smith of *The Wealth of Nations* was not "a doctrinaire advocate of laissez faire,"[11] or, as Thomas Wilson has argued this year, if it can be shown that "individualism may also be founded on sympathy,"[12] then *Das Adam Smith Problem* largely disappears. Another type of problem invented by the historians, and the main object matter of this paper, has been Smith's alleged failures to recognize "the industrial revolution" and to anticipate "the French

revolution," the two great revolutions of his day. As regards
the French revolution W.R. Scott has argued that "the plan of
The Wealth of Nations did not require a reference to the
development of events in France and thus there was no reason
to make any definite forecast about them," but also that
"There is reason to believe that Adam Smith was not ignorant
as to the way in which the situation was likely to develop."[13]
After all, Smith had lived in France, both in Paris and in the
provinces, knew the most famous French economists, had
studied French public finance, and had used his extensive
knowledge of France copiously in *The Wealth of Nations*.[14]
But what about the industrial revolution? How aware was
Smith that he was living in an era of remarkable economic
expansion? Or, more generally, what can be said about "Adam
Smith and the Industrial Revolution"?[15]

Adam Smith's life coincided with the origins and beginnings
of the industrial revolution, both in England and in Scotland.
One implication could be that he had some direct role in that
great event. But Smith was neither entrepreneur nor politician,
and played no active role in the economic changes of his times.
He was, during his lifetime, a professor, a tutor, a writer and a
civil servant, and only in the last employment could he have
had any direct influence on economy. As a civil servant, however, as one of the Commissioners for Customs in Scotland,
his public work was administrative and judicial, concerned
only indirectly with economic activity or with the determination
of economic policy. Indeed, no case can be made for Smith's
active participation in the eighteenth-century British economy,
and little for his influence on contemporary policy affecting
that economy.[16] If Smith is to be associated with the
industrial revolution, it must be in some other way. And there
are, I think, two meaningful ways in which this can be done:
(a) to determine Smith's *awareness* of "the industrial
revolution" and his analysis of it; (b) to determine Smith's
influence, the role of his ideas in the making and sustaining
of the industrial revolution, particularly the impact of his
theories of individual freedom on economic policy. These

relationships have been already the subject of historical inquiry, with varying interpretations, and have been generalized into what seems to be a modern conventional wisdom. The traditional view, as expressed by J. Bonar in Palgrave's *Dictionary,* was that "He [Smith] was conscious not indeed of being on the eve of a revolution, but of being in the full progress of a revolution that had dawned some time before him."[17] Recent historians have thought differently: R. Koebner has argued of *The Wealth of Nations* that "there was not a line in [Smith's] book anticipating such transformations as were to take place," and M. Blaug, also, that "there is nothing in the book to suggest that Adam Smith was aware that he was living in times of unusual economic activity."[18] On influence, also, views have changed. Smith, once thought to be "the great apostle of laissez-faire,"[19] "a genius . . . destined, not only to extend the boundaries of science, but to enlighten and reform the commercial policy of Europe,"[20] has been converted into a modified supporter of intervention, whose qualified laissez-faire statements have been used out of context to rationalize liberal beliefs rather than to cause them.[21]

In contrast with such modern interpretations, I take the nineteenth-century view of Adam Smith, that he was aware of the economic changes occurring in his lifetime, that his policy prescriptions were directed towards increasing economic growth, and that his influence, particularly his inspiration of, and theoretical justification for, liberal economic policies, and hence for the remarkable economic growth of the nineteenth century, was considerable. He was not aware of "the industrial revolution," as that term is used by many modern historians; that would have been impossible. He was aware of economic growth and he explained how and why it occurred; that was a remarkable achievement.

III

The argument that Adam Smith was unaware of the industrial revolution rests basically on three propositions: (a) that the timing and character of "the industrial revolution" was such that he should have been aware of it; (b) that he was writing on subjects, especially in *The Wealth of Nations,* that were essentially concerned with industrialization; and yet, (c) that there is no evidence in his writing of awareness of the industrial revolution. All three propositions are of doubtful validity: (a) the first depends on incorrect views of what the character of eighteenth-century economic change was— emphasizing technological change rather than economic growth—and of when the industrial revolution began—before rather than after Smith's death; (b) the second depends on an incorrect view of Smith's intentions in writing *The Wealth of Nations,* a view that incorrectly shifts the focus of attention to industrialization, whereas Smith was concerned primarily with establishing the outlines of a new science, and with explaining "the wealth of nations"; and (c) the third depends on ignoring the extensive evidence of Smith's awareness of eighteenth-century economic change in *The Wealth of Nations* and other writings, and in his library, his correspondence, his travel, his social and intellectual life, and his career. Adam Smith was no recluse, and he knew and corresponded with a wide variety of prominent people, not only scholars like himself, but "men of affairs." Many of the examples he used in his writing, especially in *The Wealth of Nations,* came from travel and discussion, discussion not only with politicians but with businessmen. He had the good fortune not only to have travelled widely but to have resided for long periods in Glasgow, Edinburgh, London and Paris at a time of remarkable intellectual excitement, and in those cities to have belonged to a number of clubs, societies and salons where discussion of economic affairs was a leading activity. Smith, in consequence, was extremely well informed about the world in which he lived, and used that world constantly to exemplify his economic theories. "No book was ever written," wrote J.S. Nicholson of *The Wealth of Nations,* "in which theory was more constantly brought to the test of fact."[22]

On the timing and character of the industrial revolution, there is disagreement among the historians, although the

1780s is now a widely accepted starting decade, and increasingly the industrial revolution is seen as an example, the first example, of sustained economic growth through industrialization.

The Wealth of Nations was published in 1776, and was written over the previous twenty-five years; it was written, therefore, while the industrial revolution was in the making and was published only at a time when technical and economic change were accelerating. The long-term consequences of industrialization were only slowly realised—how much awareness of industrialization can be found, for example, in David Ricardo's *On the Principles of Political Economy and Taxation,* or, in another context, in the novels of Jane Austen?— and it would have been impossible for Adam Smith, even in the last years of his life in Edinburgh, to have been aware of more than the modest beginnings of industrialization in Scotland[23] and the first decade of substantial industrial growth in England. What Smith did live through, recognized and explained, was "the nature and causes of the *increasing* wealth of Britain," the economic growth that preceded large-scale industrialization but which included much industrial development. He also recognized and explained growth elsewhere in the world, especially in the British colonies in North America, and lack of growth elsewhere, for example in China. The changes Smith witnessed are ill-described as "the industrial revolution"—a term, in any case, invented by a Frenchman in the 1820s, popularized by an Englishman in the 1880s, and in common use only in the twentieth century.[24] It was, rather, slow but sustained economic growth, balanced and widespread, embracing both agriculture and industry, and affecting most areas of Britain, including Scotland.[25] Some of this change has been described by some historians as revolutionary—hence the revolutions, agricultural, financial, commercial and transportation, which allegedly preceded the industrial revolution— but only in an age of excess in which the word revolution has lost its force and clarity, and in which every change in economy and society has become "revolutionary." Smith was certainly unaware of such revolutions; but to argue that he was unaware of revolutions that many modern historians do not recognize, was unaware of the industrial revolution that had barely begun during his lifetime, and did not anticipate later scholarship, is surely unreasonable. In any case, *The Wealth of Nations,* the volume in which awareness of industrialization would have occurred if anywhere in Smith's writings, was not a book, in its interests or coverage, to require recognition of industrialization; and when Smith refers in it to industry it is by way of example, not to analyse industrialization as a phenomenon in the industrial revolution sense. Moreover, only the third and fourth editions of the 1780s, the last corrected by Adam Smith, could have had much to say about industrializaton.

IV

The evidence of Adam Smith's awareness of eighteenth-century growth can be divided conveniently into five sections, concerned respectively with (a) his travel and observation, (b) his clubs and discussion, (c) his association with business men and politicians, (d) his library and (e) his writings.[26] Each section deserves extended treatment, although here each will be discussed only briefly. The combined impression of Adam Smith from this evidence is of a man not only well-schooled and well-read, but widely-travelled and in association with some of his most important contemporaries, both in Britain and in France, and, also, of a man in continuous debate about the leading economic and political issues of the day. It is implausible, therefore, to argue that Smith was unaware of the changing character of the eighteenth-century economy. And even if the evidence from his life and career, and his library, cannot decisively prove awareness, but only suggest its near certainty, the evidence from his writings is quite decisive.

(a) *Travel and Observation.* Smith, for his times, travelled widely, and resided for relatively long periods in six important cities—Glasgow, Oxford, Edinburgh, London, Paris and Toulouse; he also resided briefly in Geneva, Bordeaux and Montpellier, and for much of his life, in Kirkcaldy. Residence in each of these cities, and travel within Britain and France, gave him insights into contemporary economy, and provided examples freely used in *The Wealth of Nations.*[27] It also gave his analysis a realistic and comparative flavour, with its interesting examples from contemporary life, and its telling comparisons between Scotland, England and France.[28] Residence in France undoubtedly gave Smith a vital broadening of education and experience, as whole sections of *The Wealth of Nations* demonstrate. In Smith's own Index to *The Wealth of Nations,* France has one of the longest entries (along with agriculture, colonies, corn, labour, revenue and trade), and in the Cannan edition, where the Smith entries are expanded by more comprehensive indexing, France has the longest entry. But all of Smith's travels and experiences are used to illustrate *The Wealth of Nations,* and examples from his personal observations enliven almost every page, whether discoursing on the relative nutritional merits of wheaten bread, oatmeal and potatoes,[29] on universities,[30] on the grocery trade,[31] or on fertility and infantile mortality.[32] It is quite impossible to read *The Wealth of Nations* without recognizing that much of its description of politics, society and economy arose directly from Smith's own experiences, enriched by his reading and his intellect.

(b) *Clubs and Discussion.* Smith's disposition, according to J.R. McCulloch, "was social in the extreme, especially in his own house, and in the company of his early friends. His Sunday suppers were long celebrated in Edinburgh circles."[33] His life was full of friendship and company, and he sought, wherever he was, those clubs, debating societies, discussion groups and salons which were a characteristic feature of eighteenth-century social and intellectual life.[34] In Glasgow he was a member of Andrew Cochrane's Political Economy Club and Simpson's Club; in Edinburgh, of the Philosophical Society, of The Select Society (formed in 1754, "partly a debating society for the discussion of topics of the day, and partly a patriotic society for the promotion of the arts, sciences and manufactures of Scotland") and of The Poker Club; and in London, of the famous Literary Club of Johnson, Burke and Reynolds; and this list is not complete. Smith, also, was admitted to the Royal Society in 1773, and was a founding member of the Edinburgh Society in 1783. During his visit to Paris in 1766 he was a regular guest at most of the famous salons, and this was a year of great literary activity among French economists. In the salons of Baron d'Holbach, Helvetius, Madame de Geoffrin, Comtesse de Boufflers, and Mademoiselle l'Espinasse, and probably Madam Necker, Smith met Turgot, Quesnay, Morellet, Diderot, D'Alambert, Necker, Dupont de Nemours and Mercier de la Riviere.

It is obvious that many of Smith's leisure hours from 1750 to 1790 were spent in discussion, much of which was concerned with economic affairs, and much of which was followed by correspondence. "The great majority of the questions debated" at the Select Society, for example, "were of an economic or political character—questions about outdoor relief, entail, banking, linen export bounties, whisky duties, foundling hospitals, whether the institution of slavery be advantageous to the free. And whether a union with Ireland would be advantageous to Great Britain."[35] In Paris, also, his discussions were often, if not mainly, on economic subjects, with Necker, for example, or with Abbe Morellet with whom he discussed "the theory of commerce, public credit, and the various points in the great work which Smith was then meditating."[36] In Edinburgh, in his last years, Smith's closest friends were Black, the chemist, and Hulton, the geologist, with whom he founded the Oyster Club, which met weekly for pleasure and discussion, often about economics. The club derived from its founders, according to John Playfair, one of its members, "an extraordinary degree of vivacity and interest," and visiting dignitaries attended its meetings as one of the entertainments of Edinburgh.[37] It was, indeed, a lively community in which Smith lived his last years, a city to which, Gibbon declared, "taste and philosophy seemed to have retired from the smoke and hurry of the immense capital of London."[38] And prominent in that philosophising, discussing and debating was Adam Smith.

(c) *Business Men and Politicians.* Smith's friends were not just professors, but businessmen, politicians, farmers, printers, doctors, lawyers, architects, teachers, clergymen, soldiers,

sailors, artists, civil servants and writers. If Smith's writings
prove the broad range of his interests, his friendships, correspondence and clubs expand those interests to cover every
conceivable intellectual and topical problem of the eighteenth
century. Thus, the comment of Sir John Pringle, reported by
Boswell, that "Dr. Smith, who had never been in trade, could
not be expected to write well on that subject, any more than a
lawyer on physic," deserved a different answer from the famous
reply of Johnson.[39] Smith may not have been in trade, but he
knew tradesmen, he knew a lot about trade and related matters,
and he knew important politicians who were concerned with
trade and economy. His closest association with businessmen
was during his professorship in Glasgow, when he was friendly
with, for example, Andrew Cochrane. It was at this time, James
Ritchie, a prominent Clyde merchant, told Dugald Stewart,
that Smith converted many of Glasgow's leading merchants to
free trade.[40] After Glasgow, Smith's association with businessmen lessened, while his association with other men of affairs,
especially politicians, increased. This was partly a matter of
geography; Edinburgh gave him less opportunity for business
contacts than Glasgow, whose period of great growth was
beginning while Smith lived there. Glasgow was becoming, in
Smith's lifetime, "an industrial revolution town" which Edinburgh never became. Living in both cities, however, led him to
generalise about the character of cities, arguing that "the
residence of a few spirited merchants is a much better thing
for the common people of a place than the residence of a
court."[41] Smith's understanding of practical affairs can be
seen not only directly, as in his work in the 1750s as college
administrator in Glasgow,[42] but also in his comments on
contemporary enterprises—for example, in his hard-headed and
essentially correct comment in 1787 on the British Society for
Extending the Fisheries that "he looked for no other consequence from the scheme than the entire loss of every shilling
that should be expended on it."[43]

Smith's list of political friends is long and distinguished:
it included James Oswald, Lord Kames, Sir William Pulteney,
William Eden (Lord Auckland), the Earl of Shelburne,

Charles Townshend, Earl Stanhope, Sir John Sinclair, the Earl of Lauderdale, Henry Dundas (Lord Melville), William Wilberforce, Edmund Burke, H. Addington (Lord Sidmouth) and William Pitt, in Britain; and the Duke of Richelieu, the Abbe Colbert, Turgot, Necker and Mercier de la Rivière, in France. On his visit to London in 1787, for example, Smith dined with Pitt, was consulted by Wilberforce, and had a remarkably bad ode written to him by Addington.[44] On at least two occasions Smith was consulted directly about government policy, on the proposal for free trade with Ireland in 1779, when his views were sought by various members of the government, and on the American Intercourse Bill in 1783, when Eden approached him for advice.[45] Smith was undoubtedly flattered by the attention of politicians (for example, of Pitt), but his comments on them, and on the art of politics, were as realistic as his comments on business. His opinion of Necker, for example, was that he was "too simple-minded for a practical statesman, too prone, as noble natures often are, to underrate the selfishness, stupidity, and prejudice that prevail in the world and resist the course of just and rational reform."[46] And on the art of politics he argued of the statesman, that "he will accommodate, as well as he can, his public arrangements to the confirmed habits and prejudices of the people, and will remedy, as well as he can, the inconveniences which may flow from the want of those regulations which the people are averse to submit to. When he cannot establish the right, he will not disdain to ameliorate the wrong; but, like Solon, when he cannot establish the best system of laws, he will endeavour to establish the best that the people will bear."[47]

(d) *Smith's Library.* J.S. Nicholson reckoned that "Smith was probably one of the most widely read men of his time in all departments of science and literature."[48] This breadth of knowledge can be documented from his writing, and was reflected in his library. Fortunately, a large part of Smith's library has been identified. Not only did he leave a catalogue of his library in 1781—some 1,120 entries (2,300 volumes)— but his habit of book-plating has allowed Bonar and Mizuta to identify, from surviving collections, some 1,600 titles (over 3,000 volumes).[49] The coverage in languages and content is impressive. Of the identified volumes, a little more than a third are in English, about a third in French, and about a third in Latin, Greek and Italian. In subject range, there are five broad categories of about equal size: literature and art; Latin and Greek classics; science and philosophy; law, politics and bio- graphy; and economics and history. The number of books on travel and poetry is large; there is practically no prose fiction or theology. Of the books from his library quoted by Smith in his published writings, the majority date from after 1750; excluding the classics, a fairly complete examination of the authors referred to, either in *The Theory of Moral Sentiments* or *The Wealth of Nations,* shows that only about a quarter of them were published before 1750, and that more than a half were published for the first time after 1750. The use of economists, both living and dead, in Smith's writing is particu- larly extensive, and his library contained most of the important authors on political economy: for example, Anderson, Can- tillon, Chalmers, Child, Davenant, Gee, Hume, Law, Locke, de la Rivière, Morellet, Postlethwayte, Mun, Necker, Quesnay and Tucker. Smith's library, indeed, indicates a widely-read man, and one who kept up to date with the latest publications (many volumes date from the late seventies and eighties), and his writings prove the extensive use of the library for evidence and quotation. Smith would have had to have ignored his books to have been unaware of the changes of the eighteenth century, and this, we know, he did not do. He used his library, and he loved it. As he said to Smellie, "I am a beau in nothing but my books."[50]

V

(e) *Smith's Writings.* The trouble with Adam Smith, for the scholar who seeks to understand him, is where to begin. Dugald Stewart's account of Smith's Glasgow lectures,[51] the subse- quent discovery and publication of *Lectures on Justice, Police, Revenue and Arms* in 1896 and of *Lectures on Rhetoric and*

Belles Lettres in 1963, the more recent discovery and pending publication of *Lectures on Jurisprudence,*[52] and the intentions expressed in the last sentences of *The Theory of Moral Sentiments,*[53] clearly reveal the grand plan of Smith's intellectual endeavours. Although Smith never completed "the vast intellectual task he set himself," the volume of printed and unprinted material that has survived is formidable: in addition to *The Theory of Moral Sentiments* and *The Wealth of Nations,* his published work included articles in *The Edinburgh Review* (one on Johnson's *Dictionary*), a pioneering study in linguistics ("Considerations concerning the First Formation of Languages"), and several "Essays on Philosophical Subjects" (on the histories of astronomy, ancient physics, ancient logic and metaphysics; on the imitative arts; on the external senses; and finally, on English and Italian verbs). Thus Smith's work ranges over economics, history, politics and law, as well as into many areas of philosophy, science and the arts, and also into psychology and linguistics. And who knows what was in the sixteen volumes of manuscripts burnt, on Smith's instructions, shortly before his death.[54] Smith had the good fortune to have belonged to the last generation of universal scholars, men like Hume and Voltaire; to have lived at a time when a man as able as he was could comprehend a large part of existing human knowledge, and when the intellectuals of Europe, using that term broadly, were still a small enough group numerically for many of them to know each other, to correspond with each other regularly, and even to visit each other occasionally. Smith was a much honoured member of that group, as his correspondence, and his reception in Toulouse, Geneva, Paris and London, testify. He was in the best tradition of classical humanism, in a generation in which scholars could still assume a common heritage, largely literary and classical, but enriched with the vigorous new interests of the eighteenth century.

It is not difficult, mainly from evidence from *The Wealth of Nations,* to show that Smith was aware of eighteenth-century economic change, approved of it and explained it. He saw that change as growth, the advance of the whole economy, as for

example when he noted recent English progress: "The annual
produce of the land and labour of England . . . is certainly much
greater than it was, a little more than a century ago, at the
restoration of Charles II."[55] He saw similar progress in the
British colonies in North America, attributing it to "plenty of
good land, and liberty to manage their own affairs their own
way."[56] Smith recognised, also, not only differences in levels
of wealth between countries, but differences in rates of growth.
"Great Britain is certainly one of the richest countries in
Europe, while Spain and Portugal are perhaps among the most
beggarly."[57] And Great Britain had the greatest potential for
growth: "England, on account of the natural fertility of the
soil, of the great extent of the sea-coast in proportion to that
of the whole country, and of the many navigable rivers which
run through it, and afford the conveniency of water carriage
to some of the most inland parts of it, is perhaps as well fitted
by nature as any large country in Europe, to be the seat of
foreign commerce, and manufactures for distant sale, and of
all the improvements which these can occasion. From the
beginning to the reign of Elizabeth too, the English legislature
has been peculiarly attentive to the interests of commerce and
manufactures, and in reality there is no country in Europe,
Holland itself not excepted, of which the law is upon the whole,
more favourable to this sort of industry. Commerce and manufactures have accordingly been continually advancing during
all this period."[58]

Progress, in the modern sense of rises in per capita real
income, had been particularly marked in the eighteenth
century. "In Great Britain the real recompense of labour . . .
the real quantities of the necessaries and conveniences of life
which are given to the labourer, has increased considerably
during the course of the present century."[59] It was, he noted,
the same with the British colonies: "there are no colonies of
which the progress has been more rapid than that of the English
in North America."[60]

Adam Smith not only recognised growth, however, he
explained why growth rates differed. His explanation was in

terms of man's desires and man's institutions, and stressed four factors: resources; human nature (especially self-interest in the sense that "an augmentation of fortune is the means by which the greater part of men propose and wish to better their condition")[61] ; the constitutional framework; and the growth mechanism. Given resources, and an appropriate constitution, Smith argued, human nature would do the rest: the free play of self-interest and "the propensity to truck, barter, and exchange" would initiate a mutually reinforcing sequence of growth, the consequence of an expanding market, capital accumulation and increasing division of labour, together leading to increased productivity and increasing wealth. The growth mechanism is described in the first three books of *The Wealth of Nations,* and the constitution appropriate for growth in the fourth and fifth books. To Smith the limiting factor in growth was always the constitution: the motivation, provided by self-interest, was timeless and universal; the barriers to growth were man-made and unnecessary, and were erected always to serve particular interests. Critical to Smith's analysis of economic progress was the conviction, amply demonstrated, that a nation's institutions—political, legal, constitutional and customary—decisively affected its capacity for creating wealth. "The uniform, constant, and uninterrupted effort of every man to better his condition, the principle from which public and national, as well as private opulence is originally derived, is frequently powerful enough to maintain the natural progress of things towards improvement, in spite both of the extravagance of government, and of the greatest errors of administration. Like the unknown principle of animal life, it frequently restores health and vigour to the constitution in spite, not only of the disease, but of the absurd prescriptions of the doctor."[62]

Differences in growth, therefore, depended on differences in institutional context. "Nations tolerably well advanced as to skill, dexterity, and judgment in the application of labour," he wrote, "have followed very different plans in the general conduct or direction of it; and those plans have not all been equally favourable to the greatness of its product."[63] The economy which prospered was the one in which there existed "the obvious and simple system of natural liberty," and in which people could feel "secure in the possession of their property."[64] North America prospered, in contrast to China or Bengal, because of a favourable constitution. "The difference between the genius of the British constitution which protects and governs North America, and that of the mercantile company which oppresses and domineers in the East Indies, cannot be better illustrated than by the different state of those countries."[65] Similarly with China, which, according to Smith, had been rich but stationary since Marco Polo: "It had perhaps even long before his time, acquired that full complement of riches which the nature of its laws and institutions permits it to acquire."[66] As regards England, he concluded that "though the profusion of government must, undoubtedly, have retarded the natural progress of England towards wealth and improvement, it has not been able to stop it. The annual produce of its land and labour is, undoubtedly, much greater at present than it was either at the restoration or the revolution. The capital, therefore, annually employed in cultivating the land, and in maintaining this labour, must likewise be greater. In the midst of all the exactions of government, this capital has been silently and gradually accumulated by the private frugality and good conduct of individuals, by their universal, continual, and uninterrupted effort to better their own condition. It is this effort, *protected by law and allowed by liberty to exert itself in the manner that is most advantageous,* which has maintained the progress of England towards opulence and improvement in almost all former times, and which, it is hoped, will do so in all future times."[67]

In the process of growth Smith laid most stress on capital accumulation and the division of labour, but he also recognised the importance of structural change, technological improvements and education. He commented, for example, on the differential progress of manufactures, trade and agriculture, and its effects. "In the opulent countries of Europe," he wrote,

"great capitals are at present employed in trade and manufactures."[68] And, indicating the relationship between industrial
progress and growth: "Our ancestors were idle for want of a
sufficient encouragement for industry."[69] And, "In a rude
state of society, there are no great mercantile or manufacturing
capitals."[70]

Smith also noted the differential rate of growth of industries
within sectors, and identified growing industries and, for
example, the importance of coal for industrialization. "The
diminution of price has, in the course of the present and preceding century, been most remarkable in those manufactures
of which the materials are coarse metals.[71] "The price of fuel
has so important an influence upon that of labour," Smith
wrote, "that all over Great Britain manufactures have confined
themselves principally to the coal countries."[72]

In technological change and education, Smith saw the possibility of improving the quality of fixed capital and human
capital. "The productive poweis of the number of labourers
cannot be increased, but in consequence of some addition and
improvement to those machines and instruments which facilitate and abridge labour; or of a more proper division and
distribution of labour."[73] On education Smith stressed social
rather than economic advantage—"A man without the proper
use of the intellectual faculties of a man, is, if possible, more
contemptible than even a coward, and seems to be mutilated
and deformed in a still more important part of the character
of human nature"[74]—and linked the acquisition of necessary
social and economic skills with an education partly subsidised
by the state.[75]

As Smith was aware of growth, so he welcomed it, writing
approvingly of "the progressive state" in which "the condition
of the labouring poor, of the great body of the people, seem
to be the happiest and the most comfortable."[76] "Servants,
labourers, and workmen in different kinds," he wrote, "make
up the far greater part of every great political society. But
what improves the circumstances of the greater part can never
be regarded as an inconveniency to the whole. No society can

surely be flourishing and happy, of which the far greater part of
the members are poor and miserable."[77] He concluded: "The
progressive state is in reality the cheerful and hearty state to all
the different orders of society. The stationary is dull; the
declining, melancholy."[78]

VI

I think that I have shown that Adam Smith was aware of the
economic growth that was occurring in the eighteenth century,
indeed that he was concerned primarily in *The Wealth of
Nations* with explaining it in both economic and institutional
terms. That his knowledge and understanding were not complete is not surprising; that his ability to foresee the future
was not perfect makes him like all other economists. But, for
example, he did recognise already in 1776, or before, that
Britain's potential for growth was greater than that of other
European economies, and he did define public policies that
would ensure continued and even greater progress. But how
influential was Smith? To answer that question would require
another paper, which would consist of three parts: identifying
Smith's policy prescriptions (especially as regards market organization and the role of government); determining the extent to
which such policies were adopted in various countries, and
isolating Smith's influence as against the influence of other
policy prescribers and the effective pressure of those active
in the economy to change policy; and, finally, determining
whether or not the more liberal policies, usually attributed to
the influence of Smith, did actually promote the remarkable
economic growth of the nineteenth century. That Adam Smith
prescribed a policy of economic liberalism cannot be seriously
disputed; only a perverse misreading of Book V can lead to any
other conclusion.[79] That the various economies of Europe,
those that successfully grew, adopted more liberal consti-
tutions and economic policies in the nineteenth century is also
undoubted. That, in justification of those policies, Smith's
name was frequently invoked, is also true. In some cases, the
link seems direct and influential; for example, in Prussia,
where, according to C.W. Hasek, "the initial reforms of

economic life [were] due in large part to the stimulus of Smithian thought."[80] In other cases, the link seems obvious but less provable; for example, in the more liberal constitutional and civil codes in Europe which followed the French Code of 1804 and which generally enshrined "property and liberty" as unassailable principles.[81] That liberalism was important in releasing remarkable economic initiative and energy, and hence economic growth, is also hardly to be doubted; even those who do not like the industrial revolution and the world it produced, rarely deny its economic success. At least in justification of economic liberalism, particularly in his insistence on the sufficiency of self-interest as the proper basis of economic and political policy, and in his distrust of government, Adam Smith was, and I hope remains, influential.

NOTES

1. See the two papers of G. Warren Nutter, "Adam Smith and the American Revolution," Mont Pelerin Society Meeting, St. Andrews, 1976; and "Political Economy in the American Revolutionary Period," American Economic Association Meeting, Atlantic City, 1976: "The American Revolution thus marked the birth of a liberal political economy consistent with the principles set forth by Adam Smith, including the role he envisaged for government."

2. See D. North, *The Economic Growth of the United States, 1790-1860* (New York: Norton, 1966).

3. David Hume to Adam Smith, 1 April 1776. Quoted in John Rae, *Life of Adam Smith* (London: Macmillan, 1895), p. 286. Gibbon wrote the same day to Adam Ferguson: "What an excellent work is that with which our common friend Mr. Adam Smith has enriched the public! An extensive science in a simple book, and the most profound ideas expressed in the most perspicuous language!" Ibid., p. 287.

4. Dugald Stewart, "Account of the Life and Writings of Adam Smith, LI. D.," read to the Royal Society of Edinburgh, 21 January and 18 March 1793. Republished in *The Works of Adam Smith*, LI.D., ed. Dugald Stewart, 5 vols., (London, 1811-12). Stewart was referring, in particular, to the commercial treaty with France.

5. H.T. Buckle, *History of Civilization in England* (London: Longmans, Green and Co., 1902 ed.), vol. 1, p. 214.

6. Quoted by T.W. Hutchinson, *A Review of Economic Doctrines, 1870-1929* (Oxford University Press, 1953), p. 5.

7. A. Toynbee, *Lectures on the Industrial Revolution of the Eighteenth Century in England* (London: Longmans, Green and Co., 1908 ed.), p. 204.

8. "English School of Political Economy," *Dictionary of Political Economy,* edited by R.H. Inglis Palgrave (London: Macmillan, 1901 ed.) vol. 1, p. 733.

9. See R.M. Hartwell, "Adam Smith in Britain," Mont Pelerin Society Meeting, St. Andrews, 1976.

10. The main problems and some modern contributors have been: (1) *Das Adam Smith Problem,* J. Viner and T. Wilson; (2) Smith's failure to realize that individuals could be as self-interested about politics as the market, G. Stigler, E. West, N. Rosenberg; (3) the policy implications of Book V—laissez faire or intervention, J. Viner, E. West, A. Coats; (4) Smith's influence on policy, J.B. Brebner, A.J. Taylor; (5) Smith's "unawareness" of the world in which he lived, W.R. Scott, R. Koebner, M. Blaug. These problems are in addition, of course, to the problems of economic theory in Smith, especially his theory of value.

11. Jacob Viner, "Adam Smith and Laissez Faire," *Adam Smith, 1776-1926,* by J.M. Clark et al. (University of Chicago Press, 1928), p. 153.

12. Thomas Wilson, "Sympathy and Self-Interest," University of Glasgow Conference to Celebrate the Bicentennary of *The Wealth of Nations,* 2-5 April 1976.

13. W.R. Scott, *Adam Smith—An Oration* (Glasgow: Jackson, Son and Co., 1938), p. 19. A Commemoration Day address, 22 June 1938.

14. As I point out below, France has one of the largest entries in Smith's index to *The Wealth of Nations.*

15. The phrase is the title of at least one article, by R. Koebner: "Adam Smith and the Industrial Revolution," *Economic History Review* 11, 2nd ser., (April 1959): 3, and of a section of the chapter on Adam Smith in M. Blaug's *Economic Theory in Retrospect,* rev. ed. (Illinois: Irwin, Homewood, 1968), p. 39. See also, S. Hollander, *The Economics of Adam Smith* (London: Heinemann, 1973), p. 236: "Smith and the Industrial Revolution."

16. For Smith's civil service career see J. Rae, *Life of Adam Smith* (London: Macmillan, 1895), chs. 20, 21. The one occasion on which Smith came nearest to important public service was in 1772, when Pulteney recommended him to the Court of Directors of the East India Company as a member of a proposed Special Commission of Supervision "to institute a complete examination into every detail of its administration, and to exercise a certain supervision and control of the whole." But Parliament intervened, and the Commission was not formed. See Rae, ibid., pp. 254-56. On at least two other occasions Smith was consulted by members of parliament about economic policy; see below.

17. Palgrave, *Dictionary,* vol. 3, p. 422.

18. Koebner, *Adam Smith,* p. 382; Blaug, *Economic Theory,* p. 39. For a contrary view see Hollander, (*Economics,* p. 237), who delcares that Smith "did in fact recognise and deal with many of the important technological developments prior to 1776, with the significant exception of those occurring in the cotton industry."

19. A. Gray, *The Development of Economic Doctrine* (London: Longmans, Green, 1931), p. 142.

20. Stewart, *Account,* vol. 5, p. 404.

21. See, for example, L.C. Robbins, *The Theory of Economic Policy in English Political Economy* (London: Macmillan, 1952).

22. J.M. Clark, "Adam Smith and the Currents of History," in Clark et al., *Adam Smith*, p. 65; J.S. Nicholson, "Introductory Essay," *The Wealth of Nations*, edited by J.S. Nicholson (London: Nelson, 1895), p. 6.

23. The Carron Iron Works, which Smith probably visited, were founded in 1759 and a second iron works was founded in Lanarkshire in 1779; the first Scottish cotton mill was built in 1778, and expansion of the industry really commenced with the opening of New Lanark in 1786. See H. Hamilton, *An Economic History of Scotland in the Eighteenth Century* (Oxford University Press, 1963).

24. See A. Bezanson, "The Early Use of the Term Industrial Revolution," *Quarterly Journal of Economics 36* (1922): 343.

25. For discussion of the character of eighteenth-century growth, and of the industrial revolution also as growth, see R.M. Hartwell, *The Industrial Revolution and Economic Growth* (London: Methuen, 1971), especially Part 2.

26. All accounts of Adam Smith's life and career stem from Dugald Stewart's memoir, written shortly after Smith's death. That, and Rae's *Life of Adam Smith*, which drew particularly on Smith's correspondence, are the principal sources for this paper. Also useful were: J.R. McCulloch, "Life of the Author," *The Wealth of Nations*, edited by J. R. McCulloch (Edinburgh, 1849); J.E. Thorold Rogers, "Adam Smith," in *Historical Gleanings* (London: Macmillan, 1869); J.A. Farrer, *Adam Smith (1723-1790)* (London: Samson Low, 1881); R.B. Haldane, *Life of Adam Smith* (London: Walter Scott, 1887); J.S. Nicholson, "Introductory Essay," *The Wealth of Nations*, edited by J.S. Nicholson (London: Nelson, 1895); F.W. Hirst, *Adam Smith* (Macmillan, 1904); W.R. Scott, *Adam Smith as Student and Professor* (University of Glasgow, 1937); and articles by W.R. Scott. All references to *The Wealth of Nations* in this paper are from the Modern Library edition, edited by E. Cannan (New York: Random House, 1937).

27. See, for example, reference to Glasgow, Edinburgh and Paris on the difference between "court" and "mercantile" towns (*Wealth of Nations*, p. 320); to London on renting and the availability of accommodation ("I know of no capital in which a furnished apartment can be hired so cheap," ibid., p. 117); to Oxford, on the disadvantages of endowed educational institutions (ibid., pp. 717-18). The observations, in each case, come from Smith's own experiences, not from reading.

28. See, for example, the discussion on "consumable commodities" as necessaries or luxuries, according to custom: "Custom, in the same manner, has rendered leather shoes a necessary of life in England. The poorest creditable person of either sex would be ashamed to appear in public without them. In Scotland, custom has rendered them a necessary of life to the lowest order of men; but not to the same order of women, who may, without any discredit, walk about bare-footed. In France, they are necessaries neither to men or to women; the lowest rank of both sexes appearing there publicly, without any discredit, sometimes in wooden shoes, and sometimes bare-footed." Ibid., p. 822.

29. "The common people in Scotland, who are fed with oatmeal, are in general neither so strong nor so handsome as the same rank of people in England, who are fed with wheaten bread. . . . But it seems to be otherwise with potatoes. The chairmen, porters and coal-heavers in London, and those unfortunate women who live by prostitution, the strongest men and the most beautiful women perhaps in the British dominions, are said to be, the greater part of them, from the lowest rank of people in Ireland, who are generally fed with this root. No food can afford a more decisive proof of its nourishing quality, or of its being peculiarly suitable to the health of the human constitution." Ibid., pp. 160-61.

30. "In the University of Oxford, the greater part of the public professors have, for those many years, given up altogether even the pretence of teaching." Ibid., p. 718. This occurred, according to Smith, because their salaries came from endowments rather than from fees.

31. "In a small sea-port town [Kirkcaldy?] a little grocer will make forty or fifty percent upon a stock of a single hundred pounds." Adam Smith explains this by arguing that the greater part of this profit is really a wage to the grocer for work and knowledge similar to that of the great merchant.

32. "Luxury in the fair sex, while it inflames perhaps the passion for enjoyment, seems always to weaken, and frequently to destroy altogether, the powers of generation." "But poverty, though it does not prevent the generation, is extremely unfavourable to the rearing of children." "In some places [in Scotland] one half the children born die before they are four years old; in many places before they are seven; and in almost all places before they are nine or ten." Ibid., p. 79.

33. Quoted by Nicholson, "Introductory Essay" to *The Wealth of Nations*, p. 6.

34. Generally, for social activities, see Dugald Stewart and Rae. On Paris and Edinburgh, also see Hirst, *Adam Smith*, chapters 7 and 11.

35. Rae, *Life of Adam Smith*, p. 112.

36. Quoted in Rae, ibid., p. 201.

37. Quoted in Rae, ibid., p. 337. Smith took Samuel Rogers to the Oyster Club to hear Bogle, Laird of Daldowie, who so often gave "long lectures on mercantile and political subjects." Ibid., pp. 418-19.

38. Quoted by Rae, ibid., p. 325.

39. Johnson's reply was: "He is mistaken, Sir; a man who has never been engaged in trade himself may undoubtedly write well upon trade, and there is nothing which requires more to be illustrated by philosophy than trade does." *Everybody's Boswell* (London: Bell, 1930), p. 224.

40. Dugald Stewart, *Account*, p. xli. See also, W.R. Scott, "Adam Smith and the Glasgow Merchants," *Economic Journal* 44 (1934): 506-8.

41. *The Wealth of Nations*, pp. 319-20. He makes a similar comparison between Toulouse and Bordeaux.

42. W.R. Scott, *Adam Smith as Student and Professor*; Rae, *Life of Adam Smith*, chapter 6.

43. Rae, *Life of Adam Smith*, p. 408. See also Smith's comments on "the Ayr Bank" in *The Wealth of Nations*, pp. 297-300, for analysis of a contemporary economic problem.

44. Rae, *Life of Adam Smith*, pp. 405-6.
45. Ibid., chapters 23 and 26. See also, W.R. Scott, "Adam Smith at Downing Street, 1766-67," *Economic History Review* 6 (1936): 79-89.
46. Rae, *Life of Adam Smith*, p. 205.
47. *The Theory of Moral Sentiments*, p. 342.
48. Nicholson, "Introductory Essay,", p. 7.
49. J. Bonar, *A Catalogue of the Library of Adam Smith* 2nd ed., (London: Macmillan, 1932); H. Mizuta, *Adam Smith's Library. A Supplement to Bonar's Catalogue with Checklist of the Whole Library* (Cambridge University Press, 1967). See, also, T. Yanaihara, *A Full and detailed Catalogue of Books which belonged to Adam Smith, Now in the possession of the Faculty of Economics, University of Tokyo* (New York: Kelley Reprints of Economic Classics, 1966; first published 1951).
50. Rae, *Life of Adam Smith*, p. 329.
51. Stewart, *Account*, vol. 5, p. 412 *et seq.*
52. *Lectures on Justice, Police, Revenue and Arms* (given in 1763), edited by Edwin Cannan (Oxford: Clarendon Press, 1896); *Lectures on Rhetoric and Belles Lettres* (given in 1762-63), edited by J.M. Lothian (London: Thomas Nelson and Son, 1963). *The Lectures on Jurisprudence* (1762-63 and 1766) will be published in *The Glasgow Edition of the Works and Correspondence of Adam Smith.*
53. "To give an account of the general principles of law and government, and of the different revolutions they have undergone in the different ages and periods of society, not only in what concerns justice, but in what concerns police, revenue and arms, and whatever else is the object of law."
54. The incident is described by Rae, *Life of Adam Smith*, chapter 32, largely from Dugald Stewart.
55. *The Wealth of Nations*, p. 327.
56. Ibid., p. 538.
57. Ibid., p. 508.
58. Ibid., p. 393.
59. Ibid., p. 200.
60. Ibid., p. 538.
61. Ibid., p. 325.
62. Ibid., p. 326. See, also, pp. 324, 329, 408, 632.
63. Ibid., p. lix.
64. Ibid., pp. 651, 862.
65. Ibid., p. 73.
66. Ibid., p. 71.
67. Ibid., pp. 328-9. Italics mine.
68. Ibid., p. 318.
69. Ibid., p. 19.
70. Ibid., p. 863.
71. Ibid., p. 243. See, also, the remarks on "coarse wollens," p. 84.
72. Ibid., p. 825.
73. Ibid., p. 326.
74. Ibid., p. 740.

75. Ibid., p. 735 *et. seq.*

76. Ibid., p. 81.

77. Ibid., pp. 78-79.

78. Ibid., p. 81.

79. For a summary of the debate on the classical economists and public policy, see A.J. Taylor, *Laissez-faire and State Intervention in Nineteenth Century Britain* (London: Macmillan, 1972), and A.W. Coats, *The Classical Economists and Economic Policy* (London: Methuen, 1971).

80. C.W. Hasek, *The Introduction of Adam Smith's Doctrines into Germany* (New York: Columbia University, 1925), p. 149.

81. See A. Alverez et al., *The Progress of Continental Law in the Nineteenth Century* (Boston: Continental Legal History Series, 1919).

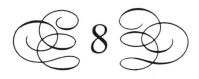

Adam Smith in
Theory and Practice

Thomas Sowell
UNIVERSITY OF CALIFORNIA, LOS ANGELES

ADAM Smith's *The Wealth of Nations* was a revolutionary event in 1776—an intellectual shot heard round the world. It attacked an economic system prevalent throughout European civilization, both in Europe itself and in the Western Hemisphere colonies. The pervasive and minute economic regulations which encrusted the British economy in the eighteenth century were widely disliked and evaded, as were similar "mercantilist" schemes of economic control in other countries. But while many people chafed or complained, it was Adam Smith who first convincingly demolished the whole conception behind these regulations, and in the process established the new field of economics.

Adam Smith not only attacked prevailing economic doctrines and practices, he attacked the political ruling powers,[1] denounced the rising economic class of capitalists,[2] opposed the creation of a British Empire,[3] and invariably sided with the "underdogs" whenever he took sides between rich and poor,[4] between businessmen and their employees,[5] or between masters and slaves.[6] *The Wealth of Nations* is such a classic that it suffers the fate of many classics: it is seldom read, though frequently mentioned—usually in the light of later concerns, rather than in the historical context in which it was actually written. Some modern writers have even tried to make Smith an apologist for the status quo.[7] But no one writes a 900-page book to say how satisifed he is with the way things are going. *The Wealth of Nations* was an attack on the status quo, and no one was more scathing in his denunciations of businessmen than was Adam Smith—not even Karl Marx.

If Smith was a revolutionary, what was the nature of his revolution, what is its present status, and how does it compare with other revolutions in other times and places? To answer such questions, it is necessary to consider both the theory and practice of the system that Smith attacked, as well as the theory and practice of Adam Smith himself. It is necessary to consider the role of *The Wealth of Nations* in the development of economics and its broader role in the social policies of its era and the succeeding two centuries to the present.

1. THE ERA OF MERCANTILISM

"Mercantilism" is a sweeping label covering a wide range of writings, laws, and policies beginning in various European nation-states in the seventeenth century, still pervasive in the middle of the eighteenth century, and never completely extinguished till the present day. The mercantilist writers were a motley collection of businessmen, pamphleteers, and politicians, and the doctrines they promoted reflected ordinary common-sense conceptions of wealth and of how an economy should function—conceptions not subjected to any of the systematic dissection or dialectic scrutiny characteristic of the medieval Scholastics before them or the professional economists after them.

At the heart of mercantilism was a conception of wealth in purely invidious or competitive terms. Wealth, to the mercantilists, was something obtained at the expense of someone else—a differential gain, like winning a race.[8] A whole society could advance its economic interests only "at the expense of other societies." The cardinal rule of mercantilism was to sell more to foreigners than you buy,[9] acquiring gold to cover the balance.[10] It is only "the treasure which is brought to the realm by the ballance of our foreign trade" which constitutes the amount "by which we are enriched."[11]

While the mercantilists exhorted their respective countrymen to buy domestic products rather than imported goods,[12] the goal of an export surplus was pursued by an array of governmental policies as well. These policies included not only direct controls over imports and exports, but also innumerable indirect measures, designed to, or alleged to, promote the same result. For example, wages were kept low through maximum wage laws, in order to lower production costs and help domestic producers to undersell foreign competitors in the world market. Prices were controlled to create a consumption pattern suited to the government's desires and beliefs. The children of the poor were assigned to learn occupations in which they were "needed," according to similar criteria. In this atmosphere, special interest groups were able to obtain all sorts of governmental favors, from direct price-fixing to an exclusion of competitors, under the blanket rationale of promoting the national interest through economic controls.

The magnitude and scope of the controls under mercantilism probably exceeded anything seen in the twentieth century, either in capitalist economies or in most socialist economies. In short, Adam Smith arrived on the scene at a time when he could observe the consequences of mercantilism as it existed in practice, rather than seeing only the theory of mercantilism as envisioned by its advocates. But while the mercantilist scheme of regulation was increasingly unacceptable and unenforceable, there was no clear alternative, nor any clear conception of what was wrong with its basic approach. Smith provided both.

The full title of Smith's classic was *An Inquiry into the Nature and Causes of the Wealth of Nations*. It was necessary to begin with the very nature of wealth, for the whole mercantilist philosophy was built on a fundamental misconception of wealth. To Smith, wealth consisted of real goods and services, and a nation was rich or poor according to its annual production in proportion to its population.[13] This changed everything. If wealth was not a fixed stock of gold but a variable flow of goods, there was no need for international contention over the division of the world's gold, for all nations could grow wealthier at the same time by concentrating on making production more efficient. Implicit also in this was Smith's conception of the "nation" as the aggregate of its people and of their well-being as national prosperity. By contrast, mercantilistic concepts of the wealth of a nation tended to amount to the power of the national government in general, and in particular its power to wage war on other national governments.[14] Since power is by its nature relative, the political goals of the mercantilists were the strengthening of their nation with respect to other nations. But Smith rejected the "malignant jealousy and envy" between nations[15] as a basis for policy. He said:

France and England may each of them have some reason to dread the increase of the naval and military power of the other; but for either of them to envy the internal happiness and prosperity of the other, the cultivation of its lands, the advancement of its manufactures, the increase of its commerce, the security and number of its ports and harbours, its proficiency in all the liberal arts and sciences, is surely beneath the dignity of two such great nations. These are the real improvements of the world we live in. Mankind are benefitted, human nature is ennobled by them.[16]

Smith differed from the prevailing mercantilist doctrine, not only on the meaning of wealth and of national prosperity, but on the very idea of what constituted the nation. Implicit in the mercantilist writings and practices was a conception of the nation as the upper classes, the bearers of its culture and property. Thus wages should be kept low to promote the prosperity of the nation. But to Smith wage-earners are the great majority of every society, and "no society can be flourishing and happy, of which the far greater part of its members are poor and miserable." This view of the nation as coextensive with its population was by no means universally accepted in Smith's time, either in Europe or America, and even in the middle of the next century John Stuart Mill could still say, "When they say country, read aristocracy, and you will never be far from the truth."[17]

Egalitarianism is pervasive in Smith. A philosopher is innately no different from a common laborer, though "the vanity of the philosopher is willing to acknowledge scarce any resemblance."[18] Smith deplored the "disposition to admire, and almost to worship the rich and the powerful"[19] and observed that the desire for prominence is the purpose "of half the labours of human life."[20] *The Wealth of Nations* denounced "merchants and manufacturers" whose "mean rapacity" and "monopolizing spirit"[21] led them "on many occasions" to "deceive and even to oppress the public."[22] Such people "seldom meet together, even for merriment and diversion, but the conversation ends in a conspiracy against the public, or in some contrivance to raise prices."[23] Smith had no higher opinion of "that insidious and crafty animal, vulgarly called a statesman or politician," whose concerns were always about the short run—"the momentary fluctuations of affairs."[24] Smith observed:

It is the highest impertinence and presumption. . . in kings and ministers, to pretend to watch over the economy of private people. . . . They are themselves always, and without exception, the greatest spendthrifts in the society. If their own extravagance does not ruin the state, that of their subjects never will.[25]

But, unlike some other egalitarians, Smith did not sentimentalize "the people." The mass was no better and no worse than the elite. Wars, for example, were not foisted on the public by evil leaders, but were popular adventures:

In great empires the people who live in the capital, and in the provinces remote from the scene of action, feel, many of them, scarce any inconveniency from the war; but enjoy, at their ease, the amusement of reading in the newspapers the exploits of their own fleets and armies. . . . They are commonly dissatisfied with the return of peace, which puts an end to their amusement, and to a thousand visionary hopes of conquest and national glory, from a longer continuation of the war.[26]

In short, to Smith we are all sinners. None is so noble or so wise as to dictate to others. In contrast to the mercantilist picture of the able statesman brilliantly planning the economic affairs of the nation,[27] Smith depicts politicians as dominated and intimidated by special interests, so powerful that "like an overgrown standing army," they have become dangerous to the government itself.[28]

Mercantilism concentrated on the *transfer* of wealth while Smith and classical economics in general concentrated on the *production* of wealth. For the mercantilists imperialism[29] and even slavery[30] were considered both acceptable and effective means of promoting national wealth. For Smith, neither was acceptable and neither was effective. While imperialism produced gains for a few businessmen and colonial officials, this was greatly outweighed by the costs paid by the taxpayers to maintain an empire. To Smith, "great fleets and armies . . . acquire nothing which can compensate the expense of maintaining them."[31] *The Wealth of Nations* closes with a plea for Britain to put aside thoughts of the glories of an empire and accommodate herself "to the real mediocrity of her circumstances."[32] Slavery was for Smith as economically inefficient as it was morally repugnant, and its existence was explained by man's need to "domineer" rather than by economic principles.[33]

Smith not only rejected the policies and practices of the mercantilists, their concept of wealth, and of the nation, he also approached the whole problem of order in the world from a different perspective. The mercantilists were part of a long tradition—still with us today—which assumes that there would be chaos in the absence of a premeditated order imposed by the wise few on the foolish many. During the centuries through which this tradition has endured, the basis for the designs of the few has ranged from the divine right of kings to the inspired ideals of revolutionaries, but the various versions of this tradition incorporate similar assumptions about human beings and about the reasoning process. Smith had very modest expectations concerning people and concerning the power of sheer reasoning to impose itself on a complex system of changing relationships. Yet he saw no chaos in the absence of such heroic feats of the intellect and will. Human society evolves its own balances much like the ecological systems of nature. That balance reflected the desires and experience of the many rather than the inspiration of the few. All general principles were formed from "experience and induction"[34] not from scholastic abstractions, "artificial definitions" and elaborate technicalities, which were capable only of "extinguishing whatever degree of good sense there may be in any moral or metaphysical doctrine."[35] In short, prosperity and progress would come not from the brilliance of an elite but from knowledge and experience which were widely diffused. In this context, the attempt of political "leadership" to impose its schemes on the economy were both uncalled for and harmful:

> The statesman, who should attempt to direct private people in what manner they ought to employ their capitals, would not only load himself with a most unnecessary attention, but assume an authority which could safely be trusted, not only to no single person, but to no council or senate whatever, and which would no where be so dangerous as in the hands of a man who had folly and presumption enough to fancy himself fit to exercise it.[36]

In a politically uncontrolled economy, the efforts of each to better himself led to that distribution of capital, labor, and land which maximized their respective returns by maximizing the value of the output to the public. Each "intends only his own gain," but in the end he "promotes that of society," though this "was no part of his intention."[37] Each individual "in his local situation" knows the economic potential of his assets and what sort of goods are "likely to be of the greatest value" far better than "any statesman or lawgiver"[38] can know from a distance.

In rejecting mercantilism, Smith rejected more generally one of the broad traditions of western social thought. Years before he wrote *The Wealth of Nations* Smith denounced the "man of system" who is "enamored of his own ideal plan of government" and who "seems to imagine that he can arrange the different members of a great society, with as much ease as the hand arranges the different pieces on a chess-board."[39] This rejected a whole way of thinking which went as far back as Plato's philosopher-king ("of all political speculators, sovereign princes are the most dangerous"[40]) and as far into the future as twentieth-century revolutionaries and dictators.

Smith's preference for market processes over political processes, as a means of coordinating a complex economy, was not based on any faith that market processes were perfect. They were merely considered superior to political processes. Moreover, Smith recognized what economists today call "external costs"—that is, costs imposed upon third parties outside the decision-making units that created these costs. Smith's general preference for "natural liberty" did not prevent him from opposing "the natural liberty of a few individuals, which might endanger the security of the whole society."[41] He supported both fire regulations and banking regulations for this reason. Smith also supported government endeavors in areas where social purposes required it but where private capital seemed unlikely to be forthcoming.[42] Education was one such area[43] — especially "the education of the common people."[44]

2. CLASSICAL ECONOMICS

Adam Smith was not simply a social thinker but the founder of an enduring school, and indeed, of a whole new area of human knowledge and analysis. Men had written on economics before, not only about contemporary problems but also about general economic principles. There was even a school of economists in France—the Physiocrats—before *The Wealth of Nations* but they were virtually forgotten a decade after they were in vogue. By contrast, Smith's work became the foundation on which succeeding generations of economists built. Even warring factions among later economists—Sismondi versus Say, Malthus versus Ricardo—invoked his name and cited his work to support their respective positions on theory and policy. Indeed, anticipations of economic doctrines attributed to later economists can be found in *The Wealth of Nations:* Say's Law,[45] the "Ricardian" theory of rent,[46] and the "Malthusian" population theory,[47] for example. Scholars have pointed out that some of these theories go back even before Adam Smith, and have questioned his originality on that basis.[48] But Smith's great treatise, like most landmarks in human thinking, is in part a synthesis of disparate elements, and its originality lay partly in the new configuration of pre-existing analytical principles and their organization into a whole new view of the world. In the same way, most of the principles behind the airplane were well known before the Wright Brothers.

Smith changed the focus of economic thinking from the marketing emphasized by the mercantilists, to the *production* of goods, and in particular to the costs of production and therefore to economic efficiency. *The Wealth of Nations* treated the division of labor as the great source of efficiency in production. Each worker, specializing in his own part of the production process, would become faster and more adept at his task. Internationally, the division of labor caused each nation to specialize in what it could produce more cheaply. Both domestically and internationally, the division of labor was limited only by the size of the market for the resulting output.[49] In a small local market, the output of one man, devoting himself to one aspect of the production process, may exceed what is saleable. A carpenter in a small rural community may do every kind of carpentry and woodwork,[50] rather than specialize in one kind of carpentry, as someone in a large city could do. Therefore, limited markets limit the subdivision of productive tasks and thereby limit efficiency. While some limits on the size of markets are unavoidable, due to transportation costs, for example, artificial limits reduce the markets—and therefore efficiency—more than they have to be reduced. These artificial restrictions range from restrictive licenses for entering some occupations to restrictions on the free movement of international trade.

Free international trade promotes low-cost production by "opening a more extensive market" for a quantity of output "which may exceed the home consumption" if the division of labor is carried out as far as the state of technology will permit. The discovery of America enriched Europe, not by the gold found in the new world, but by "opening a new and inexhaustible market" which allowed "new divisions of labor and improvements of art" which "could never have taken place" for lack of a large enough market otherwise.[51]

In keeping with Smith's general picture of an order arising from spontaneous interactions, the division of labor was not the result of any premeditated design or "human wisdom,"[52] but resulted instead from a natural "propensity to truck, barter, and exchange" goods. These exchanges tended to take place at ratios determined by the goods' respective costs of production—*not* out of a sense of fairness, or for any other philosophical reason, but because costs of production determined the respective supply prices, and goods continued to be supplied only when these supply prices were paid. The supply prices of goods were in turn the result—and sum—of the supply prices of the factor inputs that produced these goods—that is, the supply prices of labor, capital, and land.

Demand played a negligible or passive role in this analysis simply because costs were implicitly conceived of as constant with respect to output, despite Smith's discussions of how they varied with the quantity of output—i.e., how the division of labor was limited by the extent of the market.[53] Apparently there were conceived to be different possible levels of constant costs, corresponding to different methods of organizing the production of various discrete quantities of output—as distinguished from the more modern idea of continuously variable costs of production with respect to output. Still, Smith's general discussion of value proceeded as if there were a single cost of production for each good and as if value corresponded to that cost. "Effectual" demand was the quantity demanded at a price which covered "the" cost of production per unit.[54]

The role of supply and demand in Smith became the role of supply and demand in later classical economics. Supply and demand were universal *mechanisms* determining the rise and fall of price, whether in the short run ("market" price) or the long run ("natural" price).[55] However, the level around which these fluctuations took place was determined by the cost of production. The *principle* determining price was different from the *mechanism* determining price. The principle operated in the long run, when there was free competition. The mechanism operated at all times, whether in competitive markets with continuously variable supply, or in monopolistic markets, or markets with fixed supply. Supply and demand as a mechanism determining value was compatible with any principle of value-determination, whether utility or cost of production. Later, Ricardo would write to Malthus: "You say supply and demand regulates value. This, I think is saying nothing,"[56] because it is equally compatible with one theory or another. Looked at another way, to say that price was determined solely by supply and demand was to say that there was no determinant principle at work, but only a mechanism.[57]

Smith had not only a *theory* of value but a *measure* of value. While the theory of the relative value of *individual* goods had long-run prices determined by the cost of production, the measure of value attempted to compare changing *aggregate* output over time according to the differing quantities of labor which these various aggregates could command. The measure of value translated changing mixtures of heterogeneous goods into a single index of subjective well-being. Assuming the disutility of work to be constant over time, Smith measured the corresponding utility of goods by the amount of work that people were willing to endure to obtain the goods:

Equal quantities of labour, at all times and places, may be said to be of equal value to the labourer. In his ordinary state of health, strength and spirits; in the ordinary degree of his skill and dexterity, he must always lay down the same portion of his ease, his liberty, and his happiness. The price which he pays must always be the same, whatever may be the quantity of goods which he receives in return for it. Of these, indeed, it may sometimes purchase a greater and sometimes a smaller quantity; but it is their value which varies, not that of the labour which purchases them.[58]

Smith's attempt to establish a single index of heterogenous output, and to justify that index philosophically, provided later classical economists with a basis for much confusion. It appeared to Ricardo, for example, that Smith had two theories of value—one based on cost of production (ultimately labor cost) and another based on labor command.[59] But a measure of value is not a theory of value. A theory can be right or wrong, but a measure is definitional, and may only be useful or not. No substantive testable proposition in *The Wealth of Nations* would be different if Smith had chosen a different index of economic well-being. More generally, Smith's introduction of a measure of value alongside his theory of value set the stage for a similar duality in later classical economists—and for later confusions by interpreters.[60] Perhaps the classic case is Marxian value, where a measure of value by labor time exists alongside a theory of value determined by costs of production (labor and non-labor).[61]

As a theoretician, Smith was eclectic, and was little concerned with elegance, with fine points, or with appearances of consistency. Smith disparaged system-building, the reduction of doctrines to "scholastic or technical" systems of "artificial definitions, divisions, and subdivisions."[62] He was very consistent in his use of terms throughout any given chain of reasoning, so that his conclusions were unaffected by his inconsistent use of terms between one set of reasoning and another. Smith's shifting use of terms provided many pitfalls for later classical writers—but Smith himself did not fall into these pits. Thus "real" was sometimes defined in terms of goods and services[63] and sometimes in terms of labor command.[64] Rent was sometimes a residual determined by price,[65] and sometimes a price-determining factor cost[66] —but correctly used in each context. Unlike Ricardo, Smith did not always reason in terms of a one-product agriculture, whose land "rent" was a residual, but sometimes considered cases in which agricultural land had to be bid away from alternative uses, and therefore where the "rent" in one use became a cost-determining supply price in alternative uses.[67]

As a pioneer establishing a new field, Smith had the task of establishing a theoretical foundation and a structure of concepts to define the terms of thinking on the subject for those who would follow. At the same time, as a man advocating particular policies in his own time, Smith had to be concerned with the practice as well as the theory of economics. There was no indication in *The Wealth of Nations* of any confusion or conflict between these two roles. Similarly, theoretical analysis was enriched with vast factual knowledge and a gift for striking examples. The arid theoretical system-building of a Ricardo and the rambling empiricism of Malthus were equally foreign to Adam Smith. This can be seen especially clearly in these three economists' different approaches to wage-determination.

Malthus' population theory established the notion of a "subsistence" wage—whether physically or culturally determined—above which population would grow and below which population would decline. Moreover, the *rate* at which population could grow was also specified as greater than the rate at which food and other subsistence goods could increase, so that a static level of wages and a population whose observable growth rate must approximate that of the food supply were corollaries of the Malthusian theory. But despite the vast quantities of statistical and historical data which appeared in the second (and later) editions of Malthus' *Essay on the Principle of Population,* these hypotheses were never tested. The empirical material was used to *illustrate*—not test—the Malthusian doctrine. In Malthus' own words, "The principle object of the present essay is to examine the effects of one great cause."[68] History would "elucidate the manner" in which the population principle operated,[69] not test its validity. *Any* particular population found to exist in any place or time was consistent with the Malthusian theory: "The natural tendency to increase is everywhere so great that it will generally be easy to account for the height at which the population is found in any country."[70] But to "account for" facts *ex post* is not to test a theory.

Ricardo was even more cavalier. He simply *postulated* that wages were at a subsistence level,[71] and proceeded to work out the implications of this postulate, in the context of his general theoretical system. He noted in passing that wages were not in fact at subsistence,[72] but this had no effect on his analysis. Indeed, wage-determination was not a concern of the Ricardian system. Real wages were important in that system only because diminishing returns in agriculture meant a rising cost of producing a constant real wage, ultimately reducing the profit rate and bringing on the "stationary state." If real wages were also rising over time, the same result followed *a fortiori*.

For Adam Smith, real wages were important to explain, in and of themselves, and theories of wages were to be systematically tested against observable facts. He posed several straightforward tests of the subsistence wage hypothesis. The principle behind these tests was that the cost of living varied substantially from time to time and from region to region, and if wages did not vary in the same pattern, then places with the higher money wages and/or lower living costs must have real wages which are above subsistence. Following this approach, Smith found that (1) living costs were higher in the winter (because of fuel needs) while wages were higher in the summer,[73] (2) although "the price of provisions" generally varies from year to year and even from month to month, "in many places the money price of labour remains uniformly the same sometimes for half a century together,"[74] (3) regional money wage differentials exceeded regional cost of living differentials,[75] and (4) money wage variations "in place or time" are "frequently quite opposite" to variations in the cost of living.[76] In short, to Adam Smith, hypotheses about the general wage level were subject to empirical verification. Such hypotheses were not self-justifying theories, which could only be *illustrated* by facts, a la Malthus, nor were they mere convenient postulates, as in Ricardo.

Smith's own wage theories were crucial for setting the framework of classical economic policy concerns for the next century. Like Malthus after him, Smith postulated some culturally-determined "subsistence" wage, with wages above that level causing population to increase and wages below that level causing population to decrease. Unlike Malthus, Smith did not take the fatal step of postulating the *rate* of population increase, either absolutely or relative to the rate of increase of the food supply. He did recognize that those relative rates determined whether the workers' standard of living rose or fell over time,[77] but for Smith both outcomes were possible. Everything depended on how fast the demand for labor was increasing over time, which in turn depended upon how fast the country was growing. It was not in the richest countries, but in the fastest growing countries, that wages were highest.[78] Given that population would grow whenever wages were above the "subsistence" level, any stationary demand for labor would ultimately be supplied at subsistence wages. But as long as economic growth out-paced population growth, wages could remain above subsistence indefinitely. Smith's postulate of a direct relationship between wages and population, and his theory of wage determination therefore yielded observable predictions which he verified empirically. A growing country like his own had higher wages than a stationary country like China, which he believed to be wealthier.[79] By the same token, England had lower wages than a faster-growing country like America, which he believed to be not as rich as England.[80]

Because the rate of growth determined whether the bulk of the population of a nation would be economically well-off or miserable, the maintenance of the on-going growth process became the central policy concern to Smith and to later classical economics. This pervasive concern for economic growth dominated every aspect of classical economics—not only its policy positions on such issues as international free trade (especially in grain) or fiscal policy (the growth-dampening effects of a large national debt[81]), but also dominated and shaped its choice of theoretical problems and the approach to them. For example, money was discussed in terms of whether or not the quantity of money influenced long-run economic growth: It did not, according to classical economics, and money was therefore merely a "veil" obscuring the operation of real variables[82]—even though these same classical economists plainly acknowledged the short-run economic consequences of changes in monetary variables.[83] The wide-ranging controversies over Say's Law, which raged for more than two decades, were essentially disputes about the effects of thrift on economic growth.[84] Even Ricardo's narrow perception of economics as a study of the functional distribution of income[85] was geared to changes over time in that distribution in response to growth, and how such changes might tend in turn to end that growth. Smith, in short, provided the agenda of classical economics, as well as providing many of its basic concepts and theories.

The authority of Smith in later classical economics is shown by the fact that nineteenth-century dissenters from the contemporary classical tradition nevertheless based themselves on *The Wealth of Nations* and often represented themselves as the true followers of Adam Smith opposing heretics now in the ascendancy. Malthus' attack on Say's Law argued that supply does *not* always equal demand, when demand means "effectual demand" as Smith defined it[86] —quantity demanded *at cost-covering prices*,[87] (with "cost" also implicitly conceived in Smithian terms as *ex ante* supply prices rather than *ex post* factor payments[88]). Sismondi's attacks on the Ricardians' abstract, deductive method,[89] and their virtually exclusive reliance on comparative statics,[90] held up Smith as a methodological model,[91] incorporating both theory and empiricism, employing logic and history. Even Marx considered Smith's theoretical inconsistencies "justified" historically.[92]

3. THE ENDURING LEGACY

It was suggested at the outset that *The Wealth of Nations* was a revolutionary event. It represented a contemporary intellectual revolution because it attacked a prevailing scheme of thought and practice and sought to root out both the policies and the misconceptions behind those policies. It was therefore more than just a reform. Whether the changes sought were sufficiently far-reaching or fast-paced enough to be called a "revolution" depends upon what is conceived to be a revolution.

The American revolution, which occurred in the same year as publication of *The Wealth of Nations,* was very different from the French Revolution of the same era. The French Revolution was faster, more violent—and more short-lived. It was based more on abstract principles, on abstract speculation about the nature of man and the potentiality of government as an instrument of human improvement. Smith was much more in the tradition of the American revolution—more based on historical experience of the limitations of man as he is, of government's shortcomings as actually observed, and above all, a rejection of the idea that anyone has either such wisdom or such nobility as to wield the unbridled power to shape and direct his fellow-creatures. The American political system of checks and balances and the classical economists' consumer sovereignty in the market are both based on a rejection of uncontrolled power for either political or economic leaders. Both systems put in the hand of the mass of ordinary people the ultimate power to thwart or topple those who assume arbitrary decision-making powers.

Most so-called "revolutions" and revolutionaries seek primarily to change the *cast of characters* who are to wield unbridled power, and change the forms and rhetoric accompanying such power. Smith and the founders of the American republic rejected the whole idea of such power being so concentrated and so unchecked. Powerful traditions, going back thousands of years—at least as far back as Plato—advocated such unchecked sovereignty and differed only in determining the persons and the manner of exercising this power, or the principles which they should use as guides. The depth and scope of the rejection of such long-lived and widespread traditions can well be considered revolutionary in the broad history of the human race.

In terms of methods or mechanisms of change, Smith was clearly *not* revolutionary. The man of "humanity and benevolence," he said, will "content himself with moderating" those evils which he "cannot annihilate without violence." If he "cannot establish the right, he will not disdain to ameliorate the wrong."[93] By contrast the doctrinaire will insist on establishing his Utopia "in all its parts" and "in spite of all opposition."[94] Yet it is not clear that the attempt to create change "at all cost" leads to more actual change in the long run. The resistance to such methods may keep the society "in the highest degree of disorder."[95] In the twentieth century especially, we now know that societies will ultimately submit to dictatorship rather than tolerate disorder indefinitely. And though the dictatorship may continue to use the rhetoric and some of the appearances of the revolution, the kind of society actually existing may be a mockery of the original revolutionary doctrine. Certainly Karl Marx did not suffer through years of poverty to produce his doctrine in order that Stalin could send Solzhenitsin to a prison camp. More generally, such consequences have followed so regularly from revolutionary methods—both before Smith's time and afterward—that it is not at all clear that politically revolutionary methods produce socially revolutionary results, as distinguished from a change in the cast of characters in governments. Therefore Smith's doctrines may have had more long-run revolutionary potential than the doctrines of those who sought short-cuts to power. In history as in travel, short-cuts often end up taking longer to reach the destination. The concentration of power after a revolution is an obvious factor retarding further social changes, while diffused power permits continuing changes, of ultimately unlimited magnitude. The America of today is socially vastly different from colonial America. It is not clear that the Soviet Union of today is socially equally different from Czarist Russia, or even that the differences that do exist are in the direction envisioned by Marxian philosophy.[96]

Whether or not Smith's way of thinking can be classified as revolutionary, it continues to be embattled. There are still those for whom chaos seems the only alternative to an imposed economic order. The great, ambiguous phrase, "planning," increasingly appears, not only among socialists but among more politically centrist groups alarmed about some actual or possible "crisis." Smith was very skeptical about the alarms of his own time, even more skeptical of those who would save us from disaster, and had great faith in the capacity of society to accommodate. Once informed after a national setback that "The nation is ruined," Smith complacently replied: "There is a great deal of ruin in a nation."[97] As for so-called "planning," Smith was quite clear that planning goes on all the time in a market economy.[98] The only question was whether this planning should be done by individuals intimately familiar with specific economic circumstances and personally liable to lose or gain by the accuracy of their knowledge, or by distant politicians who could not possibly have equal familiarity or equal incentives. To Smith it seemed unlikely that the "artificial direction" given to the economic efforts of society would be better than the direction it would have taken "of its own accord."[99] But here, as elsewhere in *The Wealth of Nations,* the question was ultimately not one of theory but of fact.

History showed that governments habitually mismanaged economic affairs,[100] that such mismanagement was difficult to correct[101] (in contrast to the market's swift correction by bankruptcy), and that the whole bias of government projects was toward things that were big and showy rather than useful. A government will often create works "of splendour and magnificence" to be seen by those whose applause will flatter its vanity and promote its political interests, but will neglect "a great number of little works" which may have "extreme utility" but present no "great appearance" to "excite . . . the admiration" of passers-by.[102] Down through the centuries, governments have been prone to operate at a deficit, often using tricky fiscal devices to conceal just how much they were in debt.[103] With all his vast historical knowledge, Smith could not find "a single instance" where a government had actually paid off its debts in full. Every instance where a government debt had been liquidated was a liquidation by bankruptcy—either an open bankruptcy or a "pretended repayment" in devalued money.[104] "Almost all states. . . ancient as well as modern . . .have, upon some occasions, played this very juggling trick."[105]

As already noted, Smith had a low opinion of the honesty and integrity of businessmen, but they at least were forced to compete with one another. It is *competition* which forces businessmen to have "good management. . .for the sake of self-defence."[106] A government by definition is a monopoly in certain functions. Extending that monopoly to economic affairs had dangerous consequences in itself, and bringing economic agents, such as businessmen, under the protection of the government's monopoly was doubly dangerous. The "spirit of monopoly" was high in businessmen who were adept at "sophistry" to justify government protection of their interests. The protectionist doctrine of businessmen "confounded the common sense of mankind" and those who taught this doctrine "were by no means such fools as they who believed it."[107]

Despite Adam Smith's skepticism about people's morality, he made no real effort to urge higher standards of morality. This is all the more remarkable in a man whose first fame came from a book entitled *The Theory of Moral Sentiments,* published almost twenty years before *The Wealth of Nations.* Yet even *The Theory of Moral Sentiments* was not a work of moral exhortation, but instead a cool psychological and social analysis of the origins and mechanics of morality.[108] Some scholars and critics have tried to show a conflict between the first book—in which morality was considered to be based ultimately on man's ability to imagine himself in someone else's place—and *The Wealth of Nations,* in which the central mechanism of the economic system was self-interest. But there was no conflict.

The ability to imagine oneself in someone else's place was considered by Smith to be the basis for systems of morality and law. But in neither book did Smith expect people to adhere to such systems without further pressure or coercion and in the face of temptations to take advantage of others. *The Theory of Moral Sentiments* attempted to show the derivation of moral principles. *The Wealth of Nations* attempted to explain actual behavior. There it was clear that it was not from the benevolence of the butcher that we expected meat, but from his regard to his own self-interest.[109] This did not make him amoral, but only self-regarding. In the earlier *Theory of Moral Sentiments* Smith had pointed out that no one is utterly selfless, but he also noted that even the worst of men had some regard to moral precepts and felt some shame when they violated them.[110] Neither book made men devils or angels but only strivers for self-interest held somewhat in check by public opinion, the law, and other representatives of morality. It was not a bad set of assumptions—for economic analysis or any other purpose.

NOTES

1. Adam Smith, *An Inquiry into the Nature and Causes of the Wealth of Nations* (New York: The Modern Library, 1937), pp. 329, 435.
2. Ibid., pp. 128, 249-50, 402-3, 429, 438, 579.
3. Ibid., p. 900.
4. Ibid., pp. 172, 683, 686.
5. Ibid., pp. 66-67, 97-98, 249-50.
6. "There is not a negro from the coast of Africa who does not possess a degree of magnaminity, which the soul of his sordid master is too often, scarce capable of conceiving. Fortune never exerted more cruelly her empire over mankind, than when she subjected those nations of heroes to the refuse of the jails of Europe." Adam Smith, *The Theory of Moral Sentiments* (Indianapolis: Liberty Classics, 1976), p. 337.
7. "Smith was, to be sure, an unconscious mercenary in the service of the rising capitalist class." Max Lerner, "Introduction," Adam Smith, *The Wealth of Nations*, p. ix.
8. Sir James Steuart, *Works*, vol. I, *An Inquiry into the Principles of Political Economy* (London: T. Cadell, 1805 [originally 1767]), pp. 310-12.
9. Thomas Mun, *England's Treasure by Forraign Trade* (New York: Augustus M. Kelley, 1965 [originally 1664]), p. 5.
10. Ibid., p. 21.
11. Ibid., p. 21.
12. Ibid., p. 7.
13. Adam Smith, *The Wealth of Nations*, p. lvii.
14. Jacob Viner, "Power versus Plenty as Objectives of Foreign Policy in the Seventeenth and Eighteenth Centuries," *World Politics* (October 1948), pp. 1-29; reprinted in Jacob Viner, *The Long View and the Short* (Glencoe: The Free Press, 1958), pp. 277-305.
15. Adam Smith, *The Theory of Moral Sentiments*, p. 373.
16. Ibid., p. 374.
17. John Stuart Mill, "Speech on the British Constitution," *Autobiography* (London: Oxford University Press, 1949), p. 276.
18. Adam Smith, *The Wealth of Nations*, p. 15.
19. Adam Smith, *The Theory of Moral Sentiments*, p. 126.
20. Ibid., p. 123.

21. Adam Smith, *The Wealth of Nations*, p. 460.

22. Ibid., p. 250.

23. Ibid., p. 128.

24. Ibid., p. 435.

25. Ibid., p. 329.

26. Ibid., p. 872.

27. "It is the business of a statesman to judge of the expediency of different schemes of economy, and by degrees to model the minds of his subjects so as to induce them, from the allurement of private interest, to cooperate in the execution of his plan." Steuart, *Works*, vol. 1, p. 4; ". . . nothing is impossible to an able statesman" (Ibid., p. 15); the statesman is "constantly awake" on economic matters (Ibid., p. 73), and the "great genius of Mr. de Colbert" and the "genius of Mr. Law" show them to be "born statesmen" (Ibid., p. 88).

28. Adam Smith, *The Wealth of Nations*, p. 438.

29. Wesley C. Mitchell, *Lecture Notes on Types of Economic Theory* (New York: Augustus M. Kelley, 1949), vol. 1, p. 52.

30. Steuart, *Works*, vol. 1, pp. 50-52, 337.

31. Adam Smith, *The Wealth of Nations*, p. 325.

32. Ibid., p. 900.

33. Ibid., p. 365.

34. Adam Smith, *The Theory of Moral Sentiments*, p. 505.

35. Ibid., p. 463.

36. Adam Smith, *The Wealth of Nations*, p. 423.

37. Loc. cit.

38. Loc. cit.

39. Adam Smith, *The Theory of Moral Sentiments*, p. 272.

40. Ibid., p. 273.

41. Adam Smith, *The Wealth of Nations*, p. 308.

42. Ibid., pp. 684, 714-15.

43. Ibid., pp. 736-37.

44. Ibid., p. 736.

45. Ibid., pp. 321-23, 406-7.

46. Ibid., pp. 144-46.

47. Ibid., pp. 79-80.

48. For example, J.A. Schumpeter, *History of Economic Analysis* (New York: Oxford University Press, 1954), pp. 182-85.

49. Adam Smith, *The Wealth of Nations*, chapter 3.

50. Ibid., p. 17.

51. Ibid., p. 416.

52. Ibid., p. 13.

53. Ibid., pp. 17-21, 706.

54. Ibid., p. 56.

55. Ibid., pp. 55-56, 62.

56. David Ricardo, *The Works and Correspondence of David Ricardo*, edited by Piero Sraffa (Cambridge: Cambridge University Press, 1951-55), vol. 8, p. 279.

57. See Thomas Sowell, *Classical Economics Reconsidered* (Princeton: Princeton University Press, 1974), pp. 104-5.

58. Adam Smith, *The Wealth of Nations*, p. 33.

59. Ricardo, *Works*, vol. 1, pp. 12-14.

60. Sowell, *Classical Economics*, pp. 99-103.

61. See Thomas Sowell, "Marx's *Capital* After One Hundred Years," *Canadian Journal of Economics and Political Science* (February 1967): 50-74.

62. Adam Smith, *The Theory of Moral Sentiments*, p. 463.

63. Adam Smith, *The Wealth of Nations*, pp. 70, 78.

64. Ibid., pp. 30, 33, 159, 247, 248.

65. Ibid., pp. 145-46.

66. Ibid., p. 145.

67. Ibid., pp. 145, 150, 151, 152, 159; Cf. Ricardo, *Works*, vol. 1, pp. 67-68, 327-37.

68. Thomas Robert Malthus, *An Essay on Population* (New York: E.P. Dutton & Co., 1960), vol. 1, p. 5.

69. Ibid., p. 17.

70. Ibid., p. 131.

71. Ricardo, *Works*, vol. 1, p. 93.

72. Ibid., pp. 94-95.

73. Adam Smith, *The Wealth of Nations*, p. 74.

74. Loc. cit.

75. Ibid., pp. 74-75.

76. Ibid., p. 75.

77. Ibid., pp. 69, 71.

78. Ibid., p. 69.

79. Ibid., pp. 71-72.

80. Ibid., p. 70.

81. Ibid., p. 380; Ricardo, *Works*, vol. 1, pp. 187, 247-48.

82. Sowell, *Classical Economics*, pp. 54-55.

83. Ibid., pp. 56-59.

84. Ibid., pp. 69-70.

85. Ricardo, *Works*, vol. 1, p. 5: Ibid., vol. 8, p. 278.

86. Thomas Robert Malthus, *Principles of Political Economy* (New York: Augustus M. Kelley, 1951 [originally 1832], p. 66.

87. Adam Smith, *The Wealth of Nations*, p. 56.

88. T.R. Malthus, *Definitions in Political Economy* (London: John Murray, 1827), p. 242.

89. J.C.L. Simonde de Sismondi, *Nouveaux Principes d'économie politique* (Genève - Paris: Edition Jeheber, 1953), vol. 2, p. 283.

90. Ibid., vol. 1, p. 234.

91. Ibid., pp. 63, 69.

92. Karl Marx, *Theories of Surplus Value* (New York: International Publishers, 1952), p. 202.

93. Adam Smith, *The Theory of Moral Sentiments*, p. 380.

94. Ibid., pp. 380, 381.

95. Ibid., p. 381.

96. See Thomas Sowell, "Karl Marx and the Freedom of the Individual," *Ethics* (January 1963), pp. 119-25.

97. John Rae, *The Life of Adam Smith* (London: Macmillan & Co., 1895), p. 343.

98. "Every individual is continually exerting himself to find out the most advantageous employment for whatever capital he can command." Adam Smith, *The Wealth of Nations,* p. 421.

99. Loc. cit.

100. Ibid., pp. 421, 687, 688, 689, 861, 863, 873.

101. Ibid., p. 686.

102. Ibid., p. 687.

103. Ibid., p. 867.

104. Ibid., p. 882.

105. Ibid., p. 883.

106. Ibid., p. 147.

107. Ibid., p. 461.

108. ". . . the present inquiry is not concerning a matter of right . . . but a matter of fact." Adam Smith, *The Theory of Moral Sentiments,* p. 152.

109. Adam Smith, *The Wealth of Nations,* p. 14.

110. Adam Smith, *The Theory of Moral Sentiments,* pp. 93-96.